Succeeding in the
Project
Management
Jungle

How to Manage the People Side of
Projects

Doug Russell, PMP

AMACOM

American Management Association

New York • Atlanta • Brussels • Chicago • Mexico City • San Francisco
Shanghai • Tokyo • Toronto • Washington, D.C.

Bulk discounts available. For details visit:
www.amacombooks.org/go/specialsales
Or contact special sales:
Phone: 800-250-5308
Email: specialsls@amanet.org
View all the AMACOM titles at: www.amacombooks.org

This publication is designed to provide accurate and authoritative information in regard to the subject matter covered. It is sold with the understanding that the publisher is not engaged in rendering legal, accounting, or other professional service. If legal advice or other expert assistance is required, the services of a competent professional person should be sought.

"PMI" and the PMI logo are service and trademarks of the Project Management Institute, Inc. which are registered in the United States of America and other nations; "PMP" and the PMP logo are certification marks of the Project Management Institute, Inc. which are registered in the United States of America and other nations; "PMBOK", "PM Network", and "PMI Today" are trademarks of the Project Management Institute, Inc. which are registered in the United States of America and other nations; ". . . building professionalism in project management . . ." is a trade and service mark of the Project Management Institute, Inc. which is registered in the United States of America and other nations; and the Project Management Journal logo is a trademark of the Project Management Institute, Inc.

PMI did not participate in the development of this publication and has not reviewed the content for accuracy. PMI does not endorse or otherwise sponsor this publication and makes no warranty, guarantee, or representation, expressed or implied, as to its accuracy or content. PMI does not have any financial interest in this publication, and has not contributed any financial resources.

Additionally, PMI makes no warranty, guarantee, or representation, express or implied, that the successful completion of any activity or program, or the use of any product or publication, designed to prepare candidates for the PMP® Certification Examination, will result in the completion or satisfaction of any PMP® Certification eligibility requirement or standard.

Library of Congress Cataloging-in-Publication Data

Russell, Doug.
  Succeeding in the project management jungle : how to manage the people side of projects / Doug Russell.
      p. cm.
  Includes bibliographical references and index.
  ISBN-13: 978-0-8144-1615-0
  ISBN-10: 0-8144-1615-2
  1. Project management. I. Title.
  HD69.P75R867 2011
  658.4'04—dc22

                                                                        2010033809

About AMA
American Management Association (www.amanet.org) is a world leader in talent development, advancing the skills of individuals to drive business success. Our mission is to support the goals of individuals and organizations through a complete range of products and services, including classroom and virtual seminars, webcasts, webinars, podcasts, conferences, corporate and government solutions, business books and research. AMA's approach to improving performance combines experiential learning—learning through doing—with opportunities for ongoing professional growth at every step of one's career journey.

Printing number

10 9 8 7 6 5 4 3 2 1

Contents

Acknowledgments

I OWE A HUGE DEBT of gratitude to many people. Here are as many as space allows.

This book is dedicated to three people. First and foremost is my wife, Anne, whose patience, support, and, above all, flexibility made *all* of this possible. She is my alpha and omega. The second is my Mom, who believed in me no matter what, and the third is my Dad, who inspired me and convinced me I could do anything. To Ben, Matt, and Emma: like mine, your dreams can come true.

I'm also grateful to many other people:

To Michael Snell, my agent, for seeing something in my ideas. To Bob Nirkind, my editor at AMACOM, for educating me on the realities of the publishing world. To AMACOM copy editor Jeri Famighetti, and associate editor Mike Sivilli for the finished product.

To Stavra Ketchmark—without her superb editing during the intense writing phase, this book would simply not exist. She is unbelievably good at what she does.

To John Berra, chairman of Emerson Process Group, for inspiration. Thanks also to Diana Lyle, Mr. Berra's executive administrative specialist.

To Ranjit Nair, VP of HR at Global Foundries, who connected me to several of the HR people I interviewed.

To the group of HR professionals who gave me insight into project management from their view: Mike Summers at Celanese, Marcia Silverberg at Ascension Healthcare, and Alan Sockwell at AMD.

To the National Instrument crew: Mark Finger, Raj Purushothaman, Hilary Marchbanks, and, most of all, Blake Sunshine, who made it all happen.

To Leslie Martinich: for IEEE, Overwatch, and friendship.

To the Textron gang: Tom, Randy, Cheryl, Glyn, Judy, Jon, and Jeff for giving me a chance. Celeste for the collaboration!

To the Intel team: Bret, Keith, Allison, Jennifer, Jahnara (thanks also for the Indian name primer!), Richelle, Sameena, and, of course, Terry. To the many other unnamed Intel people who shared insights on a variety of subjects. You know who you are!

To the Freescale bunch: Bill L, Ann, Gay (may she rest in peace), Brian, John, Dave, Maricela, Mike, Shannon, and Gary, all of whom influenced my approach.

To three members of the College of Executive Coaching—doctors all—headman Jeff Auerbach, Relly Nadler, and Jonathan Aronoff. They educated me greatly, which allowed me to bring some helpful ideas into the project management jungle.

To Tanya Quinn for the artwork.

This book first started out as a fiction-oriented business fable. Thanks to Hasan, Sasi, Weizhen, Minnie, Fares, Elinora, Hatham, and Sankaran, who (knowingly or not) let me gain an understanding of their unique cultures, which enabled me to craft a more believable case study in Chapters 7–11.

To Arun, Ajay, Mike, JT, Allison, Barb, Mark, Sally, Mac, and other unnamed people, for their stories and ideas.

From Ft. Meade: Dick S for Ayn Rand.

Finally, to the great coaches from the world of basketball who influenced my approach to leading project teams: Mike Krzyzewski, John Wooden, and Phil Jackson most notable among them. Basketball, as everyone knows who has ever listened to my endless analogies, is the game that most closely resembles the world of knowledge worker project teams! Dean Smith should have made the list, but I just can't do it.

Introduction

ON MY FIRST PROJECT as a manufacturing project leader, inside a company known for its paternalistic management style and for being a big early driver of the Six Sigma methodology, I was the ultimate micromanager. I trusted no one, checked on everything, wanted to make every decision. I exhausted both my team and myself. I generated the desired short-term business results but was so unpopular that I was "moved on to the next challenge" as soon as it was clear the project would succeed. No one counseled me in what I should have done differently. At that point, writing a book on how to get effective results through the use of so-called soft people skills would have been inconceivable to me. And, yet, here it is.

Succeeding in the Project Management Jungle is the product of more than twenty-five years of experience in the PM trenches, making mistakes, failing, learning, and succeeding. What I discovered along the way is that if you manage with your core principles in mind and put the people you work with at the forefront, you can create successful projects and even enjoy yourself along the way.

The last thing the world needs is yet another management process. The processes out there—Lean, Agile, Six Sigma, whatever—are fine as far as they go. But clearly they *aren't* enough, as organizations still scramble to find the magic elixir that will turn their dysfunctional, sputtering projects into high-performance machines.

The pain I have witnessed over the years as people struggle to survive in these situations has been amazing: people working more than a hundred hours a week, trying every tool and process in the world, going to all sorts of training; multihour project reviews held as management seeks to help; late-evening meetings in the senior managers' offices trying to force success. Many frustrated project managers have lost their jobs and even their careers because they were unable to deal with the jungle. It doesn't have to be that hard.

In four corporations, in multiple locations and roles, and across diverse business areas, I have generated success with my project teams by using the principles described in this book. My people-centered approach to project management is a commonsense way to drive successful business results using whatever process is being touted at the moment. *Succeeding in the Project Management Jungle* will enable you to do the same.

I created TACTILE Management to encapsulate my ideas, not as another new tool that promises to be "the answer." Your success will come from within and from understanding the needs, wants, expectations, and desires of the people around you: your customer, your management, and your team.

TACTILE Management is three things:

1. **A philosophy on the right characteristics of successful projects.** My seven characteristics—transparency, accountability, communication, trust, integrity, leadership that drives needed change, and effective business results—have worked for me. Your list may be—probably *will* be—different. But, in the end, if you determine the characteristics you value and lead through them, success will come, and not at the cost of your personal life.

2. **An acknowledgment that the expectations of people are as important as the technical requirements.** Although this may sound obvious, it contradicts the core beliefs of most technical managers. Ignore this lesson at your peril. Misread expectations can derail your project and your career faster than leaving out the latest desired functionality ever could.

3. **A simple, practical guide to dealing with the pitfalls that seem to pop up on virtually every project.** These project pitfalls are illustrated through in-the-trenches stories about real people and are accompanied by action items you can put into play *today* to get control of your runaway project—no cumbersome months-long colored belt training required.

In this book, we go step by step through the concepts you need to master these three areas. Those who understand these basic concepts have a much greater rate of success than those who don't. They don't live in a fantasyland of perfect projects, but, when they come to the bumps in the road, they have in place the team and the skills to maneuver around the danger zone.

First, in Part I, we discuss the hard realities of life in the modern workplace and the factors that go into creating the project management jungle you are up to your knees in right now. Then, in Part II, we examine in detail the seven characteristics of successful projects and how TACTILE Management will help you find your way out of the jungle to create that success in your own teams.

In Part III, we scale the Expectations Pyramid, explaining how to determine the expectations of each of your key stakeholders—your customer, your management, and your team—and why you need these essential skills to manage those expectations so that you can shape the environment in which you can thrive. In addition, we hear some real-life Tales from the Project Management Jungle, both successes and failures, using the seven characteristics of TACTILE Management to analyze what they did right or where they made a wrong turn. (Names and other identifying details have been changed occasionally at the request of the subject, but the issues faced and the decisions made are real. These are people in the weeds, just like you, fighting their way out.)

In Part IV, we go through the five process groups—initiating; planning; executing; monitoring and controlling (plus reporting, which is at least as important in my opinion); and closing—and examine how to avoid common project pitfalls as you navigate them while managing complex projects and diverse groups of people. In addition, an ongoing case study, "The Path Less Taken," tracks two fictional project management teams, one with a traditional mindset and the other with a TACTILE viewpoint, from initiating through closing of Project Alpha Omega. You'll learn exactly what TACTILE Management looks like in practice in the day-to-day combat of the modern project management jungle. In Part V, we show the happy results of doing a project the TACTILE Management way.

You've probably tried several different processes, each time hoping to find that mythical "answer," and perhaps they've worked for you occasionally. But if, like most of us who've had to get out of our cubicles and lead, you're still falling short too often and you don't know why, try focusing on the *people* who drive your project. I believe that, if you follow the principles in *Succeeding in the Project Management Jungle*, you will find the success you're looking for at work and discover the key to a balanced life at home, as well.

PART I:
The Project Management Jungle

CHAPTER 1

Welcome to the Project Management Jungle

IT IS 1:15 A.M., a Tuesday night like any other. A lone light burns inside a beautiful Tudor-style custom home on the edge of the Northwest Hills in Austin, Texas. Inside, yet another busy project manager struggles to complete his work for the day, entangled within the project management jungle. In this unrelenting, always-on, pressure-cooker environment, he juggles hundreds of e-mails per day, endless meetings that accomplish little, stakeholders with impossible expectations, and new problems that should have been foreseen before they consumed additional money, resources, and attention.

His two remaining tasks for the night are to finish up preparations for his monthly ops review with management, scheduled for the next morning, and to generate an approach on how to get his design and test functional teams to work better together. The two teams have been fighting with each other for weeks and are doing little real work to solve their issues. That meeting is tomorrow, as well, "sometime after 5:00 P.M."

Down the hall, his two gorgeous children, five and three years old, slumber away. He guiltily resolves, yet again, to take them to the park on Saturday. Or perhaps it will have to be Sunday. He did at least spend a few minutes with them earlier that evening, tossing a small basketball, before they went off to bed and he off to his Mac. His wife, hoping to spend some time with him watching a DVD together, chatting about the kids, or talking about the possibility of a vacation, has given up and gone to bed.

He sends several e-mails and then, cursing to himself, realizes that he has misplaced a key notebook. Quietly, he slips into the master bedroom to check a stack beside the bed. He glances fondly down at his dozing wife as he finds the notebook and sighs as he leaves the room. He wishes there were another way to easily lead his large project group in the complex task at hand. *So many issues,* he muses. *Got to make it happen, though. Winners do what is necessary to win.* With one last look at his wife, he thinks firmly, *There will be time for catching up on all this when the project is over.*

His cell phone rings from the study. Frustrated that he cannot finish his current tasks, he hurries to answer. It is his Asian customer, full of questions about the latest status report. Wearily, he tries to explain. He can tell his customer is not very happy with the answers.

Forty-five minutes later—not really done yet—he stops for the day, noting e-mail traffic coming in from all over the world, including places where it is even later at night. Exhausted, he falls into bed, trying not to make too much commotion. He rolls over and almost immediately drops into sleep. The alarm will go off in four short hours, and he will do it all over again.

Sound familiar? *Welcome to the project management jungle!*

Escape Is Possible from the Project Management Jungle

You may think that immense stress and a large time investment are the price of success as a project leader. But there *is* another way. In the past few years, I have led multiple teams in several companies to success without working excessive hours and while experiencing much less stress than our friend here. This book will help you do the same on your projects without going to lengthy weeklong training classes or spending massive dollars on a new process.

Sadly, success in the project management jungle is too often *not* the end result of all the effort involved. Enter "project success rate" into a Web search engine and the results are disturbing, with many studies quoting success rates of only 30 to 50 percent. Of course, the majority of studies look at myriad teams in a variety of industries and applications, and each study has its own definition of success, making it hard to find a baseline for a clear picture.

Succeeding in the Project Management Jungle is aimed primarily at active project managers who work with knowledge worker teams. The term *knowledge worker*, of course, covers a lot of territory. After all, virtually everyone in today's workplace works with some sort of data. We will focus on knowledge worker teams employed in information technology (IT), software, hardware, systems design, and other engineering or technically related applications. These professionals struggle in the project management jungle every day.

Read on to learn about five key factors that create this jungle environment. Then keep reading, and by the end of this book you will have learned how to thrive there.

What Creates the Project Management Jungle?

Billions of dollars are spent every year on tools, processes, and training. Leaders and followers work more hours than ever. More metrics with which to manage are being pumped out by the people staffing the tools and processes. So why is there not a higher success rate on team projects? "Just the way it is," you say. "The projects are hard!" Yes, they are hard, but a few key factors have become tangled together over time to create the modern project management jungle:

- ► Environmental pressures
- ► Process-of-the-month club management
- ► Global nature of teams
- ► Poor leadership training
- ► Lack of coherent direction from management

Environmental Pressures

The environmental pressures are daunting. Modern schedules are short, performance requirements are fluid and seemingly always increasing, budgets are shrinking, and the right people are expensive and hard to find. Project leaders cannot change any of this; instead, we must learn how to better deal with the reality we face.

Process-of-the-Month Club Management

In an effort to respond to environmental pressures, many organizational leaders latch onto the latest project management process fad as they cast about for a recipe for success. They adopt these new project management techniques in record numbers, hoping against hope that the new processes will drive improved results. Once upon a time it was Six Sigma; more recently, Lean and Agile are the rage. These tools and processes, and many others, are all fine and useful. New tools and processes may be different—perhaps even better—but tools do not provide solutions. Like a golfer who buys a new driver but cannot escape his same old swing, new project tools are frequently purchased and implemented within the same old organizational culture that employees cannot escape.

Many adequate tools and processes are available, and over the years I have used most of them. But I have found that the particular tools used are virtually irrelevant to any individual project's success. The real key is the way that the organization thinks and learns and the culture it creates through the use of whatever tools are implemented within teams.

The Global Nature of Teams

In technology fields, rare anymore is the team that is located entirely in one country, much less in one building. Technical people—often not the best communicators in the world—struggle with communication, roles and responsibilities, and cultural issues.

Time zone and distance differences make communications difficult. Roles and responsibilities are tough to describe, but, to put it succinctly, there is almost always a struggle about autonomy and control that rages between the nonheadquarters and headquarters employees.

Multicultural issues ultimately cause the most confusion, and a great deal of time and energy can be wasted trying to deal with them. Even seemingly innocuous factors cause problems. For example, many people like to illustrate various conversational points with analogies that are familiar to virtually everyone in their own country. Many times I have heard someone in the United States use a football analogy, for example, only to be greeted with silence from employees in China, Israel, and India.

Combining an accent on top of these cultural misconnections makes for almost comical situations. Once, on a multinational call, a man from Ireland spun a detailed sports analogy involving a local football "cloub" and an exhibition against some "Febs" from "the mainland." It took several questions to understand that the Irish were playing a team from England and that he most definitely did not like them ("Febs" being a particularly harsh name to be called).

Of course, there are more serious cultural differences. It is well known in techie circles that employees from the Far East often struggle, for a variety of reasons, to bring up problems that have occurred—perceived loss of face not the least among them. On the other hand, people from those cultures often view North Americans as pushy, while Israeli employees may view them as soft and indecisive.

Poor Leadership Training

Another factor feeding the project management jungle is that managers are not taught what it means to lead project teams so that the desired business results can be achieved through people. As Larry Bossidy, chairman and ex-CEO of Honeywell International, says in the bestselling book (with Ram Charan), *Execution: The Discipline of Getting Things Done* (Crown Business, 2002): "The people process is more important than either the strategy or operations processes. . . . To put it simply and starkly: If you don't get the people process right, you will never fulfill the potential of your business. . . . People process failures cost business untold billions of dollars."

Once, many corporations put new and recently promoted managers through effective leadership programs. GE had such a program. Motorola and many others had them as well. Some, such as Boeing Aircraft, still do, but such training is not currently prevalent, in part because of the global recession. According to an Ambient Insight Research study, "The overall U.S. corporate training and education market has been shrinking at a small but steady rate (negative 2–3% CAGR [compound annual growth rate]) since the recession of 2000–2001." What is needed is the mindset of a coach, who encourages, pokes and prods, and develops but doesn't try to control.

A related issue is the lack of formal project management training in college for many technical managers. Often people come into the workplace, become very competent at some technical specialty, and are put in charge of a small group, then increasingly larger groups until they control entire projects. The ad hoc ways they managed their small teams (e-mail, spreadsheets) will at some point cease to scale up. Without an adequate understanding of the value of project management tools and techniques, they "just don't understand," says Arun A., a Texas-based post-silicon test manager for a major semiconductor company. And what people don't understand, they tend to undervalue.

Lack of Coherent Direction from Management

Finally, there is a lack of coherent direction from above. The management leaders are often so caught up in surviving in their own jungles that they don't learn the needed coaching skills that would allow them to support their followers. Rare is the manager in the chain above you who actually mentors or coaches you, as opposed to micromanaging you.

The cartoon *Dilbert* has found great popularity by mining this vein of worker frustration with management precisely because it is so widespread. Almost everyone, unfortunately, can relate to it. Many project leaders miss the insidious interplay of these causes until they are well down a treacherous path that leads deep into the jungle, perhaps to emerge much later battered, bruised, and scarred for life.

TACTILE Management™ Defined

TACTILE Management was created in response to the question I often hear: "Why don't all the great process tools like Six Sigma, Lean, Agile, and so forth work more often?" It is true that these processes are valuable and can enable success. I was the manufacturing manager for a product that achieved Six Sigma quality in a Motorola factory, and I have seen teams successfully use many process tools. I have also seen companies abandon process tools. Process tools work better with some teams than with others, even in the same company. My conclusion is that it takes more than just process tools to generate success.

The difference is that, in the cases of success, there is always someone in the trenches who not only uses the process correctly but also has the people skills to match how the process is implemented with the capability of the team and the organization. The successful project manager:

► Creates and implements a systematic approach (philosophy, if you will) for leading people, with certain key concepts and words synthesized into a value system that creates a positive culture and enables success for the team.

► Incorporates the expectations of key stakeholder groups—the customer, management, and the team—into solutions.

► Identifies and plans for potentially perilous situations on projects. Problems occur on all projects, successful and otherwise. But avoiding or minimizing the effect of project pitfalls is key to successful completion, no matter what the process or tool might be. These pitfalls go beyond just the standard risks you might encounter.

➤ Project managers who master these three areas succeed far more often than those who do not. It is not that they don't have problems, but rather that when problems do occur they already have a cohesive team and an approach that enables them to weather the storm.

TACTILE Management is a people-based project management system. What does *people-based* really mean, you ask? Maybe a couple of quotes will bring this into focus. Rooted in my belief system is that "leaders can't motivate anyone—they can only create the environment where individuals motivate themselves," from Robert Townsend's classic 1970 business book *Up the Organization* (Jossey-Bass, 2007). I also like this from Tom DeMarco and Timothy Lister's *Peopleware: Productive Projects and Teams* (Dorset House, 1987): "Since 1979 we've been contacting whoever is left of the project staff to find out what went wrong. For the overwhelming majority of the bankrupt projects we studied, there was not a single technical issue to explain the failure. The major problems of our work are not so much technological as sociological in nature."

The world of project management is a tough, hands-on environment that requires project managers to leave their cubicles and get into the fray. It is indeed a tactile experience. People who work on projects don't have time for theory or weeks to learn yet another new process to get the job done.

The seven letters of the acronym TACTILE each correspond to a key characteristic of successful projects. Each term is defined later in this chapter and discussed thoroughly in Chapter 2.

➤ **T**ransparency
➤ **A**ccountability
➤ **C**ommunication
➤ **T**rust
➤ **I**ntegrity
➤ **L**eadership *that drives needed change*
➤ **E**xecution *results*

Attempting to create successful project teams through the use of squishy-sounding words like these is often derided as the use of soft skills. But the ability to get work done by understanding people is vastly undervalued in the project management world. As Marcia Silverberg, vice president of HR Strategic Initiatives for St. Louis–based Ascension Health, says, "Soft stuff *is* the hard stuff. Culture eats strategy for lunch."

New processes and tools, with metrics and quantitative data—the so-called hard skills—are preferred by many project managers because they seem to provide actionable data and create the appearance of positive action when implemented. Managers who put these tools into place often only appear to be doing something useful. The last thing the world needs is another process that requires certification—these cult-like saviors of process, with guardians at the gate preventing qualified people from becoming project managers because they don't know the secret password. Instead, we need commonsense solutions to the tough problems that occur on projects. I have no quarrel with these processes per se; they form valuable disciplined frames upon which projects succeed. But tool and process alone do not generate success. Six Sigma, Lean, Lean Six Sigma, Agile, Theory of Constraints, and similar programs may be great systems, but they are not enough. In TACTILE Management, the term *strong skills* is defined as the ability to use any robust process, such as Lean, Agile, or Six Sigma, combined with the ability to get results through people.

Strong skills are rooted in three concepts:

▶ Constant respect for all individuals, including individual contributors on the team, the customer, the management food chain involved in the project, and yourself, the project manager.

▶ Successful leadership through the people—customer, management, and team—involved, using whatever tool or process the organization deems appropriate.

▶ Conceptualized and articulated principals of leadership that are put into action. There are seven characteristics in the TACTILE Management system. Your own system may have more or less than seven; remember that TACTILE Management is a roadmap, not a recipe. Check out Stephen Carter's *Integrity* (Harper Perennial, 1997) to better understand creating and implementing value systems.

Other important terms within the TACTILE Management framework include the following:

► A *team* is defined as individual contributors (the hands-on workers), project managers, senior managers, and the customer (in a different role) working collaboratively toward the same overall goal in an integrity-based common culture of transparency, accountability, communication, and trust, with leadership that enables execution of the desired business result.

► The *goal* for the team is more than just meeting the schedule, cost, and performance requirements. The larger goal for teams is always to grow the capabilities of each team member, as well as of the overall team, so that the team will continue to function at a high level long after the project manager has gone on to the next assignment.

► *Success* means meeting stakeholder (customer, management, team) expectations for schedule, cost, and scope while maintaining quality, as well as ensuring that the team grows in overall capability and is a more potent force than when you joined the team.

TACTILE Management is not prescriptive; it is more about creating leadership that implements values to drive the desired behaviors than it is about the process or the toolset used. This is powerful stuff, and it should not be immediately dismissed because it is not quantitative. There are data, however! As Donald Phillips recounts in his book *Lincoln on Leadership: Executive Strategies for Tough Times* (Warner Books, 1992), "Tom Peters reported in his research that the best, most aggressive, and successful organizations were the ones that stressed integrity and trust." Of course, virtually all organizations include values of one sort or another in their mission statements, but there also can be a good deal of cynicism present within those organizations about those mission statements.

Within a few miles of my house in central Texas is a corporation, National Instruments (NI), that drives people-based values into its culture while generating strong business results. Per the corporate website, throughout its history NI has been recognized as a company that continuously develops award-winning, innovative products that help simplify the job of engineers and scientists worldwide. With off-the-shelf software such as NI LabVIEW and cost-effective modular hardware, for more than thirty years NI has transformed the way engineers and scientists design, prototype, and deploy systems for measurement, automation, and embedded applications.

Currently employing more than five thousand workers, NI truly has a people-based culture where information is shared and decisions include input from all those affected. The NI website says: "We maintain this fun and innovative corporate culture by recruiting the best and the brightest employees and motivating them in a work hard, play hard environment." According to Rajesh Purushothaman, manufacturing director, and Mark Finger, HR vice president, Dr. James Truchard, cofounder of the company, in 1976, fostered this people-based value system and it permeates every decision that is made. In essence, the culture at NI—for a tenth straight year one of *Fortune* magazine's 100 Best Companies to Work For—is all about maximizing the value of people.

And this culture generates strong business results. Per its website, NI grew revenue from $1M in 1980 to $820M in 2008. The September 2009 10-Q quarterly report showed that the company has $232 million in cash, with no debt. NI has maintained 74 to 76 percent gross margins for twenty years. This is just one example that excellent value systems can generate great results both for businesses and for people. There are other examples of businesses that drive results the TACTILE way, and we will look at them throughout the book.

Succeeding in the Project Management Jungle

Enough background—you have a project to run. To thrive as a project manager, you must succeed in all three of the following key areas:

➤ Developing the Seven Characteristics of Successful Projects
➤ Mastering the Expectations of Key Stakeholders
➤ Avoiding Project Pitfalls

Developing the Seven Characteristics of Successful Projects

It is essential that you, as a project manager, develop the philosophical underpinnings of your approach to managing your projects. To blindly jump into leading any group of people without these underpinnings will leave you like a boat at sea without a guide to shore when storms come.

In my twenty-eight-year career as a design engineer, project engineer, manufacturing manager, program manager, proposal manager, manager of program managers, director of projects, and director of systems engineering and test with Motorola Inc., Intel Corporation, Overwatch® an Operating Unit of Textron Systems, and others, I have found seven characteristics essential for successful knowledge worker projects. Some are more important than others, but, for me, all had to be present to some degree for success to occur. And they were most effective when consciously developed, in the sense of development as the means of making something new, such as a product or mental creation.

Don't misunderstand me; there is no magic here. These seven characteristics are what I found to be essential. Your list might be shorter or longer. Here is a brief definition of the seven characteristics, all of which are discussed more fully in Chapter 2:

➤ **Transparency:** The project manager's ability to ensure that the team members are told the truth about organizational policies, business climate, and decisions that affect them

► **Accountability:** The project manager's ability to ensure that everyone on the team knows and executes his or her role, feels empowered and supported in that role, knows the roles of the other team members, and acts upon the belief that those roles will be performed

► **Communication:** The project manager's ability to ensure that needed information flows quickly and seamlessly to where it can be used with optimal efficiency

► **Trust:** The project manager's ability to promote one agenda for all team members—the team's overall goal—and to create a culture in which team members believe they are being told the truth in all interactions

► **Integrity:** The project manager's ability to show team members that a consistent set of values or beliefs is being used appropriately to make the correct difficult decisions; also, his or her ability to integrate the efforts of all involved on the project toward the common goal

► **Leadership that drives needed change:** The project manager's ability to plan and execute the appropriate culture change within the team to drive the actions required for the desired business results

► **Execution results:** The project manager's ability to blend the other six characteristics to produce the desired business execution results

Each of these seven characteristics is important in any action taken as a project manager. All of them, or your equivalent list, should be planned into any approach for leading a team.

Mastering the Expectations of Key Stakeholders

One of the old warhorses in project management is the triple constraints triangle (see Figure 1-1), where the three constraints shown are time, cost, and performance (performance is often also called *requirements* or *scope*). Altering any of these three constraints requires that they be traded off against at least one of the others.

Figure 1-1: Traditional Triple Constraints Triangle

Performance (Scope)

All three cannot be improved simultaneously. For example, if you want to improve a schedule's finish date, you have to allow higher cost and/or lower performance. As is often done, *quality* has been added inside the triangle to show that quality is always required and cannot be traded off. Most project managers deal quite well with linear tradeoffs of these three technical constraints.

A Guide to the Project Management Book of Knowledge (Program Management Institute, 2004), more commonly referred to as the PMBOK® Guide, is the standard text through which the Program Management Institute (PMI) provides guidance to project management practitioners. The *PMBOK Guide* mentions that the expectations of key project stakeholders must be considered, but not how. *How,* of course, is the hard part and a key to succeeding in the project management jungle. Much complexity occurs when the expectations of your customer, management, and team are added on top of the schedule, cost, and performance technical constraints. Many project managers do not approach the problem this way, continuing to try to trade off the technical constraints, while either ignoring or caving in to the inputs from stakeholders. The inability to balance the expectations of the three stakeholder groups causes more project managers to fail than do schedule, cost, and performance issues.

Instead of a simple triangle, I prefer a Triple Expectations Pyramid (see Figure 1-2).

As shown, each face of the pyramid concerns the expectations of one of the following: your customer, your management, or your team. Each face of the pyramid is itself also a triple constraint triangle, with schedule, cost, and performance (requirement or scope) constraints. *Successfully balancing these nine constraints simultaneously is what provides the environment within which a project manager can succeed.*

Success is not simply meeting the technical goals—that is, the schedule, cost, and performance goals that were given out early in the project. Leaders doggedly do so and yet subsequently fail to thrive in their careers. This is because they do not balance the expectations of their customers, their management, and their teams with the technical goals of the project.

More powerful is the leader who may not meet all the technical requirements but still somehow thrives. Often people ascribe this success to politics or to connections. Sometimes this is true, but often something more profound has occurred. Expectations are often unspoken and possibly not fully understood even by the person with the expectations. Possessors of high emotional intelligence have a leg up on the rest of us here. Anthony Mersino's def-

Figure 1-2: Triple Expectations Pyramid

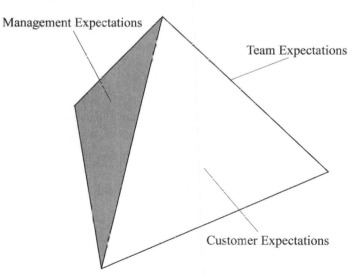

Management Expectations

Team Expectations

Customer Expectations

inition of the term, presented in his book *Emotional Intelligence for Project Managers* (AMACOM, 2007), is helpful: "Knowing and managing our own emotions and those of others for improved performance." Project leaders who develop high emotional intelligence are better able to simultaneously balance the technical requirements and these key stakeholder expectations in a way that satisfies all involved. *Develop* is the key word in the preceding sentence; turns out there is hope for all of us. This is because, unlike IQ, which seems to be fairly constant throughout one's lifetime, EQ can be learned. Many executive business coaches focus heavily on EQ with their clients, often to good effect. Methods to improve your EQ are discussed briefly in Chapter 7.

After all, successful leaders care about what customers and project team members think, so it is natural that project leaders who can incorporate the expectations of these groups into their overall project solution will be valued. Think of the sports world, another area of intense pressure where high performance is rewarded and poor performance is visibly punished. Great coaches in the sports world also successfully create winning teams in chaotic, dynamic environments with a set of diverse stakeholders they don't control. It makes sense that a leader is better appreciated if the leader can include the often-unstated expectations of these stakeholders in the final approach. Succeeding within the Expectations Pyramid is defined as *being able to balance schedule, cost, and performance goals simultaneously with the expectations of your customer, management, and team so that all parties are satisfied with the results.*

Grace, a project manager in a well-known technology company, was promoted to VP after she was able to master the Expectations Pyramid (not that she would describe it that way) on a project that was very important to her corporation and to the survival of the design center in which the project was located.

Grace took over a design center that had failed quite publicly on a previous project and was possibly in danger of being closed. Grace was able to leverage this expectation of (or at least concern about) closure into a huge personal commitment from the team. She also, for the most part, protected her design center—quite remote from the corporation's Silicon Valley headquarters—from management's addition of desired functionality (scope creep) through a single-minded intensity and focus that convinced all parties that she would succeed. Chapters 3–6 show you how to master the Expectations Pyramid on your own projects.

Avoiding Project Pitfalls

The *PMBOK Guide* is a complex process-oriented document, not a how-to manual. PMI calls it "a standards and guideline publication," with the primary purpose of identifying "that subset of Project Management Body of Knowledge that is generally recognized as good practice." More than one project leader has joked with me that there should be a book titled *A Guide to the PMBOK Guide*. In a sense, that is what Chapters 7–11 of this book are meant to be.

There are five process groups within a project: initiating, planning, executing, monitoring and controlling, and closing. Most project people refer to these five process groups as phases. PMI frowns on that phraseology, rightly pointing out that each of these process groups is done throughout the project, not just during one period. To minimize confusion and needless wordiness, I will generally refer to each process group in one of two ways: for example, initiating or initiation, instead of talking about the initiation phase or the initiation process group. As mentioned in the Introduction, I have added reporting to monitoring and controlling in this book.

On every project, project leaders encounter certain common pitfalls as they try to meet the goals of the project. For example, pitfalls are encountered when creating the project charter in initiating or in choosing the appropriate change control process in planning. Pitfalls that affect initiating, planning, executing, monitoring and controlling (and reporting), and closing are discussed in Chapters 7–11. Mastery of these pitfalls will go a long way toward enabling your success. Chapters 7–11 also contain an ongoing case study that contrasts a standard project with one managed in a TAC-TILE way and offer practical tools that you can use on your own projects.

Now that you understand the philosophy at the foundation of TAC-TILE management, let's get more specific. Chapter 2 maps out the details you need to find your way through the jungle and end up right where you want to be.

PART II:
The Foundation of TACTILE
Management

CHAPTER 2

The Seven Characteristics of Successful Projects

I OFTEN USE PATRICK LENCIONI'S *Five Dysfunctions of a Team* (Jossey-Bass, 2002) as a way to illustrate how teams work (or don't work) in the real world. I once mentioned Lencioni's book during a conversation with a local engineering leadership educator. Her reaction was different; to her, the book is too negative. She thinks he should have written about what leaders should do, not what they shouldn't do.

The statement made increasing sense as I gave it some thought. I have long felt engineers and technical people are trained to be negative. As an engineer myself, I see that we spend much of our time looking out for what may go wrong, and, even when things seem to be working well, success is never taken for granted. We just *know* there is an undiscovered failure in there somewhere!

Ted, a project manager in the western United States, was this kind of person. Ted worked with an overall program manager who resided in the Washington, D.C., area. Ted's program manager would take an early-Monday-morning flight two times zones away and arrive at Ted's plant in early midafternoon, tired and exhausted from the road. Ted, good engineer that he was, would greet his project manager at the door with the latest grim news and how it might affect the overall schedule and cost for the project.

Ted's timing aside, this is not always a bad thing. If a bridge falls down or an electrical device fails, people *can* die. Arguably, this focus may generate robust designs, but it is bad for the people involved, as they often become cynical, cranky, and unhappy—in other words, *burned out*. A positive approach to project management can help you achieve the goals of your project by showing you what works, instead of how not to fail.

The seven positive characteristics of successful projects listed in Chapter 1 form the philosophical foundation of TACTILE Management. These concepts are proven and have been applied successfully in several companies (including an insurance agency), on a variety of team types, and in several geographical locations. TACTILE Management is not a new tool or process that requires complex certification but a different way of thinking about the problems found in the project management jungle. No special colored belts or secret passwords needed here!

That's all well and good, you may be thinking, but maybe this question is nagging at you: *Why should I care?* I am well aware that people do not have time for unquantifiable concept words that do not drive results. I don't, either. After all, you are a project manager, with a complex project to run.

The question is a fair one, but here is a question for you: *Why should anyone follow your lead as project manager?* These days, knowledge workers are quite independent and readily move among companies, often because of excitement over a particular technology or project. They often are not direct reports to the project leader. The project leader cannot *make* them do anything. They likely know far more about a particular area of expertise than the project leader, so you cannot count on controlling them with technical knowledge.

Here is an answer to both questions: to be effective as a leader, one must possess a set of values that drive the needed right actions. Leaders with large numbers of motivated and talented followers are successful because *they have and act on key values that drive results.* Not having bedrock beliefs upon which to make decisions allows the leader to be manipulated from all sides.

Having a set of common values makes good business sense to John Berra, chairman of Emerson Process Management in Austin, Texas. Emerson Process Management is a large component of the $25 billion Emerson, a diversified global manufacturing and technology company, with more than 140,000 employees and approximately 255 manufacturing locations worldwide. In his role as president of Emerson Process Group (business leader is the internal name for the role), in 2004 Berra started a leadership development process that ultimately generated nineteen key competencies for leaders in his organization.

To drive the process initially, Mr. Berra sent a memo to the entire organization explaining what was coming. He then took a leadership team offsite and used the LEADERSHIP ARCHITECT Competency Suite®, licensed from Minneapolis-based Lominger International, to whittle sixty-seven competencies down to the nineteen key Emerson Process Group competencies.

The process has continued to this day. "It has become the language used internally," Mr. Berra says, "for our high-potential candidate process." A set of three leadership courses, attended by high-potential employees over a period of two years or so, accentuate business learning within the context of the key values. Real cases from Emerson history are used to anchor the desired concepts. The values also provide a general cultural foundation within the entire organization.

What were the business results? When Mr. Berra became the business leader, in 1999, the organization had sales of $3 billion; when he moved to his current role of chairman, in 2008, yearly sales were in excess of $6 billion. Mr. Berra cites this process as one of the key reasons his business was able to grow at this rate while competitors struggled to do so. Simply said, good business results come from identifying, articulating, and putting into practice your key values. It worked for Emerson and also for National Instruments, as described in Chapter 1. It can work for you.

Now, let's look in detail at each of the seven characteristics that form the TACTILE Management philosophical foundation.

Transparency

The project manager's ability to ensure that the team members are told the truth about organizational policies, business climate, and decisions that affect them

The term *transparency* is used widely in the business and political world to convey openness and clarity, when just the opposite can be true. As Warren Bennis, author of twenty-seven books and a pioneer in the field of leadership studies, mentions in *Transparency: How Leaders Create a Culture of Candor* (Jossey-Bass, 2008), "Despite the promise of transparency on so many lips, we often have the sinking feeling that we are not being told all that we need to know or have the right to know." This understandably often leaves people quite cynical about transparency, but, for the leader, modeling transparency is the easiest, quickest way to start down the road toward a cohesive and highly functioning team. This is because the leader can start creating transparency the moment the team is first assembled. The other characteristics require more time and effort.

How to quickly create transparency? Just learn what the team cares about and communicate about those things. Team members desperately want information about what matters to them and care little about other information. Deducing what information is important to them can be tricky in an organization of introverted technical people! Often, they just want to know when the breaks will be, what snacks will be offered, and where the restrooms are.

To find out what your team cares about, start by making a list of what *you* care about. Then, starting with your staff or the key functional managers for the team, ask for input. Also have skip-level one-on-one meetings with individual contributors (workers) below your staff or your direct reports. Do this in a relaxed, open way so that they do not feel pressure.

If you just cannot bring yourself to manage a probing interactive conversation, that's okay. This is not rocket science. People usually want to know about (1) how the business is doing overall, (2) how the local organization is faring in the ongoing corporate competition between sites, and (3) how the project is perceived by key stakeholders. In lieu of any information from the team members about what they want to hear, you can start with these three items and do the following:

▶ Share the information periodically in an all-hands meeting.
▶ Be ready between such meetings to answer team member questions.
▶ Dedicate a section of your staff meeting to those subjects.

How do you address sensitive areas such as potential layoffs or talk about project cancellations or site closures? These are the very subjects people want to know about, so you cannot ignore them. First, quote as fact only statements that have been made public through your organization's HR group. Start all answers with public information releases and then carefully (oh so carefully!) address areas of interest where you are on firm ground. Learn how to speak about them with truth and empathy—while protecting your organization—in a way that you would want to be communicated with, and you will be fine.

For example, many managers would refuse to address a question about a rumor about site closure. Paula, a project manager with high levels of empathy, got this exact question during an all-hands meeting at her location, far from the corporation's Chicago headquarters. Her answer: "I have heard nothing about a site closing, but of course the company has no requirement to stay here. To our credit this site shipped our new design on time, which is integral to the corporation's strategy on an important new product, so we are performing well. All we can control anyway is what each of us does and what we do as a group. Let's just keep doing it." She watched the questioner closely until she could see his body language relax. Only then did she ask a question of her own, with an earnest look and a small smile: "Does that make sense?" When he smiled slightly and nodded, she maintained eye contact for another instant and then politely asked if there were more questions.

Project and senior leaders routinely express concern about talking too often and/or sharing excessive information with teams. They are worried about the time required and the distraction of too much information and fear that the team might not want to take the time for so much communication. Lest you as a leader listen to those concerns and do nothing about transparency, ponder this. If a leader is not transparent with a team about the things the team cares about, members will spend a lot of time filling in the lack of information with their own worries and anxieties and gossip. As a result, they will work less efficiently, as the following story illustrates.

Tom, a Texas-based project controls manager for a large global technology corporation headquartered in Silicon Valley, noticed the trouble his organization had with transparency (and several other things) during a period of reorganization. The organization held all-hands meetings using an Internet call-in system that allowed presentation on myriad personal computers worldwide, with an international call-in number for audio interaction. The calls usually originated from the corporate headquarters in San Jose, California. The frequency of these all-hands meetings increased greatly during the reorganization, as leaders tried to clearly communicate the process and the details.

The employees at Tom's site would gather in a common room for the calls. To minimize background noise, it was traditional to mute telephones at the nonpresenting locations. As the corporate leaders presented information, Tom noticed just how *non*transparent was the culture within the organization. With the telephone muted, people around the room would openly speculate on what the person speaking really meant in terms of reporting relationships, organizational structure, and similar issues. Occasionally, someone in the room would un-mute the telephone and ask a question, almost always in a seemingly polite nonconfrontational way that reflected none of the feelings expressed when the phone had been muted. Tom quickly became aware that the managers in San Jose had little understanding of the real concerns and issues of the local employees. Discussion with peers at other sites revealed much the same feeling.

After the calls, many of the attendees at Tom's site, now thoroughly irritated and dismayed, would continue grumbling and rumbling through the halls on the way back to their cubicles. Those who went out to lunch—the calls typically occurred right before lunchtime in Texas—would continue to try to parse out exactly what was going on and what the presenters had really meant. Needless to say, a great deal of productive work time was lost to gossip and speculation. Tom's efforts to raise awareness around the issue went nowhere. Senior leaders were not uninterested; they were just under great time and task pressure and essentially did not know how to react to what Tom told them. The organization continued to lose a lot of productivity throughout (and after) the almost two months of reorganization.

Do not ignore transparency just because it sounds like something that needs to be done only on Wall Street or in Washington, D.C. You need to be transparent in all your interactions, lest your grumblers mute your input!

Accountability

The project manager's ability to ensure that everyone on the team knows and executes his or her role, feels empowered and supported in that role, knows the roles of the other team members, and acts upon the belief that those roles will be performed

Accountability is a misunderstood concept. Many managers act as if accountability means getting in the face of those who make mistakes to make sure they get the reaming they deserve so that they will not mess up again. Senior managers often tell project managers, "You are accountable for the project. I'll be coming to you whenever anything goes wrong." That is only half right. Accountability—to be effective—has to extend to everyone on a team. You as project leader are accountable, but so are the team members and senior management (your management food chain). Management has a different role to play, certainly, but it cannot be completely distanced from the project and expect success.

Start the process of accountability early. Accountability is all about defining roles and responsibilities for each person on the team and holding everyone to them. In one of your first conversations with team members, tell them briefly how you are going to hold yourself accountable and what you, in turn, expect of them. A carefully chosen sentence or two is all that is needed.

Call a special staff meeting the first week you take over the project (or soon after project approval if a new project), and have this discussion. Be sure you discuss roles and responsibilities with newly assigned people soon after they join the team. Roger Connors and Tom Smith, cofounders of a leading firm for accountability training, discuss an "accountability conversion" in *How Did That Happen: Holding People Accountable for Results the Positive, Principled Way* (Portfolio, 2009). You must take these actions to create the right culture on your team. If you do not, some sort of team culture *will* develop, and it may not be the one you want.

Then have a project kickoff meeting to drive your desired culture. Include a brief discussion of your key values as they apply to executing business results within the team. You should plan on spending time teaching people how to provide accountability for themselves and others in a constructive way. There may be some raised voices along the way. That is okay. Once the right culture takes hold, you will have a powerful team. A culture of mutual accountability leads to winning project teams.

Communication

The project manager's ability to ensure that needed information flows quickly and seamlessly to where it can be used with optimal efficiency

I like a team communication exercise called helium sticks. Helium sticks are extendable to something like eight feet and, as you might guess, are quite light. The exercise involves lining up a group of people shoulder to shoulder, with only people's fingertips allowed to come into contact with the stick. The stick is adjusted on everyone's fingertips until it is horizontal and then the team is told to lower the stick as low as possible without anyone losing contact with the stick and without the stick dropping down into a hook formed by fingers or into a palm so that it is more easily grasped.

The results are almost always the same: the stick *rises* and participants get upset with each other. Side by side, working on a seemingly simple task, and clearly motivated, why don't the team members work closely together to meet their goal? Team members mention the time pressure, confusion about the directions, concern that other teams are cheating, and their mounting frustration with their inability to get their helium stick to drop as reasons why they lose control of their emotions.

Welcome to the perversity of human communication! To be effective, you need to get people talking freely and openly about the right information. You do so by asking questions and actively listening. Spend some time putting yourself in their shoes and thinking like they do. Once you understand their needs and concerns, you will become a better project leader

For Arun A., our post-silicon test project manager in the semiconductor industry, communication is an essential value. His team is responsible for testing the output of a design group. If the design group doesn't understand exactly what his post-silicon test group's capabilities and constraints are, the circuit may not be testable. If problems are discovered early enough, there may be no impact, but the later in a project they are discovered, the larger their impact on cost and the greater the time to fix them. Arun has found that driving a process of constant education back and forth between all involved parties (including internal customers) is required, and he starts this communication engagement process as early as possible.

For efficient communication to occur—in other words, for information to flow from wherever it is to wherever it needs to go—accountability must already be in place, certainly by Planning. If team members know each other's roles and what is expected of each person early on, they will also know whom to talk to about different issues. People normally do not know whom to talk to about detailed issues unless this is the focus of someone in project leadership, and it is especially true on a large global project involving hundreds of employees in crash mode, that is, when many new people are being added all at once. If working-level followers cannot figure out whom to talk to about an issue, they will ask their immediate leader, who also may not know the details of other functional teams. In any case, working through a leader in this way wastes time and does not help followers learn how to work together. Your job is to get the team to work together so that needed information flows quickly and accurately. There is no time to waste.

To make all this work, your functional leaders and staff also have to learn to work together as a unit. Nick, a project manager with responsibility for a variety of different functions, taught his staff how to work together on real issues (he *didn't* send them to a class on team building) by changing the structure of weekly team meetings from boring recitations of the week's technical progress (or lack of it) to action-oriented discussions where participants explored—*as a team*—the solutions to issues that affected more than one function. The actions that ensued were then captured in SMART format: Specific, Measurable, Attainable, Realistic, and Timely. The assigned actions would be due sometime in the next week. Long-term issues were broken down into week-size chunks. The team began to work together, and Nick brought the project to a timely and successful conclusion.

The larger issue under discussion may take time to resolve, but people need short-term actions to galvanize and focus their efforts. Once your staff implements this approach, the managers in their organizations will begin to model the behavior within their teams, and you will be on your way to creating the culture you are looking for.

For more reasons than just good communication, you need to have weekly one-on-one meetings with all direct reports. The meetings are not a chance for you to beat them up or to tell them how to do their jobs but rather should be pegged to their agenda—what they want to talk about, factors that affect their ability to do assigned tasks or grow into new roles. The meetings should be geared toward helping them learn how to lead more efficiently and thoughtfully, and you should be a model for the desired behaviors. Ideally, your direct report should talk approximately 80 percent of the time. If you are talking, you are not listening.

Your role is to ask the right questions and to offer advice and direction only after your followers have exhausted ideas on what actions need to be taken. Ideally, they should also be implementing 80 percent of the action items that arise during the meeting. You should help only with problems they cannot solve themselves. Be sure that the action items you do take are high priorities on your list of things to do, people to see, and places to go. That demonstrates, through action, that their needs matter.

Trust

The project manager's ability to promote one agenda for all team members—the team's overall goal—and to create a culture in which team members believe they are being told the truth in all interactions

Trust within the team is the ultimate goal for a project manager—actually, for *any* leader. Trust comes after the leader has been implementing the preceding characteristics in the TACTILE paradigm at least reasonably well. The team will grant trust as it buys into the overall plan.

Great things occur on teams when there is trust. This is why sports teams, as well as business teams, can improve dramatically when a change in management approach occurs, as opposed to simply introducing new tools and processes. An example of this in the sports world is what Mike Krzyzewski was able to accomplish with the U.S. Olympic basketball team at the Beijing Olympics in 2008 after previous coaches and U.S. national teams had underachieved for many years. In *The Gold Standard* (Business Plus, 2009), about the 2008 Olympic experience, Krzyzewski relates his comments at the first team meeting. He said, "Two concepts are fundamental to a team dynamic: communication and trust. I don't know how we can get beat if we communicate and trust." And, of course, they were not beaten, instead winning the gold medal in convincing fashion.

But this is harder to find in the knowledge worker world. Susan Lucia Annunzio, former adjunct professor of management at the University of Chicago's Booth School of Business and president and CEO of The Center for High Performance, and colleagues surveyed three thousand knowledge workers across the world for her book *Contagious Success: Spreading High Performance Throughout Your Organization* (Portfolio, 2004). One key finding was that in order for workers to perform at peak performance, they have to be treated well and trusted. But, sadly, Ms. Annunzio's study found that only about 10 percent of knowledge worker teams are managed in the high-performance ways that can lead to these results.

Dr. Ajay C., a computer-aided design (CAD) manager for a well-known company in Austin, relates an experiment in his organization in which a large design team was split into two teams, each with the same goal. Charles managed one team in a secretive, micromanaging way; the other was led by Mike in a trusting, open, and communicative style geared toward learning. Mike was willing to share much of what his team was doing with Charles's team and still won the competition, as he listened better to the customer and to his team. Since then, Mike's responsibilities have grown, while Charles's continue to shrink.

About thirty miles southwest of San Antonio is the small town of Devine. And divine (sorry!) it is to leave the traffic and congestion of the Austin-to-San Antonio I-35 corridor and break free into a relaxed rural environment. Devine, according to its Chamber of Commerce website, is the self-proclaimed avocado capital of Central Texas and home to about ten thousand people.

One of these residents is Mark Kidd, a client of my executive coaching business for a time. Mark owns the State Farm Insurance agency in town and has been a State Farm agent for more than thirty years. Mark's easy smile tends to disarm until you see the deep intelligence that lies within.

Mark's conference room is so covered with President's Club plaques and various other honors that there is almost no room on the walls for any new awards. According to Mark, in 2009 he and his team achieved Top 250-agency status, chosen from a total of seventeen thousand total agencies nationwide.

But Mark doesn't just want to win; he wants to win the right way: "Doug, I don't need the money that comes from being a top agent I want a winning team. I want [my employees] to share in the financial part of this thing; I want them to win a trip to somewhere fun every year. I want them to learn and become better every year."

This attitude is reflected in a high-performance life. Mark was a top student at Texas A&M and, interestingly, a member of the Singing Cadets there, a difficult and highly sought-after honor. Among his six (all college-educated) children are graduates of Harvard, Dartmouth, Emory, and Georgetown; another recently returned from Moldova after two years in the Peace Corps. Asked for the qualities to which he attributes this success, he says, "Hard work. I just outworked everybody. I hired you because you mentioned integrity in a clear way. Trust is important, too. People buy insurance because they trust me and State Farm."

Indeed, trust (and integrity, another TACTILE characteristic) is a key value for State Farm itself, as the State Farm code of conduct says: "Every day each of us makes choices where integrity, honesty, and trustworthiness come into play. . . . We all have a responsibility to exercise good judgment, honesty, and integrity when performing our jobs."

Mark has this to say about trust:

Some things in life are like doors that swing both ways; for me, trust is one of those. People need to know that I trust them as well as they need to know that they can trust me. Once trust is established, interactions between the trusting parties are generally interpreted as being for the common good and edification of all members. That allows everyone to move quickly through troubling and unsettled times. When my team knows that I have their back and I know they have my back, we can work very hard and take a lot of risk—if we start to fail, we know a teammate will be there to pick us up. Once a team builds trust, they operate at a level that is amazing. Trust is built by being authentic,

empathetic, and honest without regard to someone's per-
sonal net worth. Conversely, trust is destroyed by being
duplicitous and aloof.

Mark and his team did all this in the small town of Devine, Texas. Next time you eat some guacamole, think of Devine and the Mark Kidd Insurance Agency. And think of the value of words like *integrity* and *trust*.

Integrity

The project manager's ability to show team members that a
consistent set of values or beliefs is being used appropriately
to make the correct difficult decisions; also, his or her abili-
ty to integrate the efforts of all involved on the project
toward the common goal

If a team follows your leadership, it will do so largely because of two aspects of your integrity: (1) the set of values that encapsulates what you stand for and how you make decisions, and (2) your ability to integrate the individuals on the team into a whole to help them reach their goals by achieving the team's common goal.

Integrity, along with transparency, might seem the squishiest of the squishy here. A couple of quotes may help you see it for the core strong skill it really is. As mentioned in Stephen Covey's *The 8th Habit: From Effectiveness to Greatness* (Free Press, 2005), Dwight Eisenhower, leader of the Allied Armies in the Second World War and thirty-fourth president of the United States, said, "The supreme quality for leadership is unquestionably integrity. Without it, no real success is possible, no matter whether it is on a section gang, a football field, in an army, or in an office."

Frances Hesselbein, CEO of the Leader-to-Leader Institute, couldn't be more different physically from the image we have of the imposing Eisenhower, but both see integrity in a similar way. Jim Collins, author of *Good to Great*, in the foreword to *Hesselbein on Leadership* (Jossey-Bass, 2002), states Hesselbein's cardinal rule: "If your leadership flows first and foremost from inner character and integrity of ambition, then you can justly ask people to lend themselves to your organization and your mission."

Integrity is also important to John Berra, chairman of Emerson Process Group. He talks frequently about integrity, but, perhaps more important, he models his personal sense of integrity on the quality of being *human* and on being approachable to his employees. He also uses global all-hands webcasts to drive information and consistent values throughout the organization. As he says, "The following is not original with me, but I like to say the pope has to be more Catholic than anybody else."

A code of personal integrity found in twenty-one major religions, the Golden Rule says: "Do unto others as you would have them do under you." Sally Crowell, president of Crowell Systems, a software company in Charlotte, North Carolina, says, "We built our business on the Golden Rule, and these principles have always resulted in satisfied customers and led to numerous referrals. Honesty, integrity, and looking out for the client's best interests are key. We always go the extra mile with service. For example, one of our clients sent us a dead server that was literally full of water, rust, and mold. The hard disk had crashed. The client's whole business and patient's medical records were on it. He could not access any of the data. Our technician poured the water out of it and worked hard to reboot it. Fortunately, he was successful. He worked for several days trying various methods in an effort to recover the data. Finally, he was able to retrieve the information. It was a huge save for the doctor." This is another example of how integrity is not just a squishy concept but is key to so much of what makes a business valuable to its customers.

Establish your own set of business values based on your personal integrity. You don't have to advertise your beliefs, because actions speak louder than words. In fact, it will be counterproductive if you do. Do tell your teams what your beliefs are, but then model those values in your actions and decisions. Your teams will follow you consistently, and this will generate better business results.

There is a second aspect to integrity. Yale Law professor Stephen L. Carter quotes from the *Oxford English Dictionary* in his book *Integrity* (HarperPerennial, 1997): Integrity is "the condition of having no part or element taken away or wanting; undivided or unbroken state, material wholeness, completeness, entirety." This is why the final step in putting together complicated systems, like spacecraft or microprocessors, is called integration. Even the toughest no-nonsense data-only engineering manager appreciates the value of integrity in the sense of wholeness and purity of integration.

These two meanings of integrity—*ethical/moral rules to guide decisions* and *wholeness*—taken together provide the glue that binds the previous four characteristics. You will fail if you try to implement the other characteristics without having thought out your own personal sense of integrity and without understanding that your job is the integration of individuals into a team. This is often why the introduction of new project management processes and tools fail to provide the desired results.

Leadership That Drives Needed Change

The project manager's ability to plan and execute the appropriate culture change within the team to drive the actions required for the desired business results

Good things in life do not happen without some sort of plan, certainly not on complex endeavors like a modern knowledge worker project. To make all these abstract concepts work on your team, you must plan how you are going to make it happen. That is where leadership when making culture changes comes in.

First, evaluate how much culture change is actually required to be successful. This is not a one-size-fits-all process; in fact, the greatest value in this approach comes from its flexibility. If you are taking over an existing team, ask these questions:

- ▶ Does the team have an overall team goal?
- ▶ What are the structure and agenda of staff/team meetings?
- ▶ Are all-hands meetings occurring? If so, what are the agenda and periodicity?
- ▶ How does important information move around?
- ▶ How does important information get to the project manager for monthly operations reviews with management? How

effectively is that information communicated to management? What does management do with the information?

▶ What is the approach around schedule and cost control and around metrics, headcount, and risk management? Who owns the updating of this information?

Decide which of these areas you want to change first (I suggest the overall team goal as a unifying theme), and integrate that change into an approach that incorporates the previous five TAC-TILE characteristics (or your own set of values).

Execution Results

The project manager's ability to blend the other six charac-teristics to produce the desired business execution results

Generating solid business results is why we do what we do, right? The six characteristics previously discussed, if planned and executed properly, will lead to the execution results your organization desperately craves. Knowledge worker teams do not want to hear these squishy words, so don't talk much *about* the words but, rather, *use* them as the basis for how work will get done.

In the next section, we look at using TACTILE Management characteristics to deal effectively with the hopes, fears, and aspirations of three key groups: your customer, your management food chain, and your team. I call this Expectations Management, and it is your key to succeeding in the project management jungle.

PART III:
Mastering the Expectations of Key Stakeholders

CHAPTER 3

Expectations Management

AS A PROJECT MANAGER, your key stakeholder groups are (1) your customer, (2) your management, and (3) your project team. The individuals in these three groups bring to work each day their hopes, worries, fears, dreams, and aspirations. The difficulty is that people are trained to not talk of these things, based as they are on subjective feelings. Often, people on a conscious level are not totally aware of these feelings.

In contrast, the workplace is supposed to be about data. Data are collected, collated, analyzed, synthesized, and discussed until decisions are made. Left unstated are the feelings (hopes, worries, fears, dreams, and aspirations) of those involved. These feelings set up expectations for future events that drive all sorts of actions that seemingly have little to do with the project at hand. Therefore, a type of *expectations management* is required. The expectations of your stakeholders are critical. You cannot succeed without understanding and creating strategies for dealing with them.

High-Level Stakeholder Expectations

What follows is an example of a high-level expectations analysis of these three stakeholder groups that incorporates some frequently encountered situations

▶ **Customer Expectations:** The customer (the representative of the paying entity, not the end consumer necessarily) expects the product to be delivered for the lowest cost and on schedule, with the features she was promised and/or visualizes. She is concerned that her money is being wasted and that the project is not getting the best and the brightest or the right focus within your organization. She worries that you and your management food chain aren't telling the truth. Her actions are driven by these worries and concerns, by her expectations about her fears.

▶ **Your Management Food Chain's Expectations:** Your management food chain expects to build future business with the customer; hence, it will, from your point of view, tend to appease the customer. Your project is likely only one aspect of your organization's relationship with the customer. Your supervisor expects sales and profit growth in his business area. He is concerned that the customer can't be pleased and that he may be unable—due to time or other constraints—to ensure the success of the project. He is worried that he can't trust you to protect him and the organization. These types of worries and concerns drive his subsequent actions.

▶ **Team Expectations:** The team expects to do cool, interesting, cutting-edge work. Individual team members worry that project management (you) will give in to customer and management demands that will lessen the team's creativity and, ultimately, their fun. Their actions are driven by these worries, and thus they may tend to do what they prefer rather than what they are *told* to do, especially if there is no perceived personal penalty for doing so. This makes it particularly important that project managers learn how to inclusively manage and to be able to uncover team member concerns and incorporate them into appropriate solutions.

The project manager is caught in the confluence of these triple sets of expectations. The following case study illustrates this dilemma.

Case Study: The R.101 Project

Longtime technology author James R. Chiles writes in his book *Inviting Disaster: Lessons from the Edge of Technology* (Collins Business, 2002) that Dirigible R.101, at 770 feet, was the world's longest airship when it finally got off the ground, on October 4, 1930, four years late to the original plan. The project manager was an RAF lieutenant colonel named Vincent Richmond. Richmond learned world-class airship design from the Germans; R.101 was the first dirigible command of his own. Richmond was determined to succeed. As you will see, like many recently promoted managers, Richmond evidently did not know how to manage upward; he did not know how to say *no* to management.

Expectations Analysis

Here is an expectations analysis of the Dirigible R.101 story, and a sad case it is: expectations of none of the three key stakeholder groups were met, with tragic results:

▶ **Customer expectations:** U.K. taxpayers were told by their government in 1924 that Dirigible R.101 would be in the air within two years, would carry one hundred passengers and fifty crew, would have a cruising speed of sixty-five to seventy-five miles per hour, and "would reach Egypt in three days or less, a full two weeks faster than any steamship." This was part of a plan to "bring the empire closer." There were also expectations that it would serve each branch of the military in some fashion: a submarine spotter for the Navy, a troop transport for the Army, and an aircraft carrier for the Air Force.

► **Management's expectations:** In addition to the R.101's stated goals as kind of a bus in the sky, the Air Ministry was also determined that the R.101 would be a test bed for breakthrough ideas. This merging of two such disparate and distinct top-level design goals should be chilling to you as a project manager. To meet the test bed goal, no strengthening wires were used in the framework. As a result, the designers had to make the girders heavier to ensure strength, making the R.101 a wallowing pig in the sky when it finally flew. In lifting trials, it could hoist only thirty-five tons, instead of the original goal of sixty tons. The seventeen tons of diesel engines, which had originally been designed for locomotives, were directed by Parliament (senior management indeed!). As it approached initial launch, the R.101 was leaking so much hydrogen (22,000 cubic feet per day) that it had to be lengthened to create more lift. In an effort to meet schedule expectations, only about one-half of the planned testing occurred, and testing was often undertaken only on days with no wind, a clear violation of the test plan. These (and other) concerns caused an inspector to deny the flight permit. But the Secretary of State for Air, Lord Christopher Birdwood Thomson, a well-connected and charismatic leader, drove the project to conclusion. "Safe as a house," he told the press, "except for the millionth chance."

► **Team expectations:** According to author Isabelle Royer, in the essay "Why Bad Projects Are So Hard to Kill," in the *Harvard Business Review on Managing Projects* (Harvard Business School Press, 2005), "Projects often become self-selected cheerleading squads of true believers who can become blind to problems that emerge." This was certainly true for the R.101. For example, true believer Richmond and his wife moved to a cottage close by so that he could work extra hours. Also, the team was in competition with another team, which was building something called the R.100, adding more stress and determination to the mix. The men on the project team seemed keenly aware of the risks. They just apparently had no desire to stand in the project's way. After all, they had worked on the project for several years and expected to see their hard work actually fly.

Execution Results

Project manager Richmond and Lord Thomson were among the forty-eight dead (out of fifty-four aboard) when the dirigible crashed in gusting winds above the Bois des Coutumes hills, just a few miles into France and only a few hours after taking off on its maiden voyage.

Traditional Project Constraints with Stakeholder Expectations

As mentioned in Chapter 1, the triple constraints triangle (see Figure 1-1 on page 16) is a standard tool in project management. Most project managers, left alone and not micromanaged, deal quite well with the linear tradeoffs of the three technical constraints of time, cost, and scope. But, at its most fundamental level, the triple constraint triangle uses those three constraints as mechanical levers, as if pulling them alone will create the desired results. Minimized (or ignored) are *people* and how to work through them for success.

Much complexity is created when the expectations of your customer, management, and team are added to the technical constraints imposed by the requirements of schedule, cost, and performance (scope). Many project managers continue to try to trade off the technical constraints, while either ignoring or caving in to the expectations of their stakeholders. When failure occurs, the root cause is almost always connected somehow with a failure to discover and then meet the expectations of the three key stakeholder groups.

Traditional project management tools and techniques are not up to dealing with the expectations of these key stakeholder groups. A methodology like Lean, with a goal of efficiency and value from the customer's viewpoint, is a move in the right direction, but only for part of the right reason. Agile methodology, as discussed in Jim Highsmith's *Agile Project Management* (Addison-Wesley, 2004), comes closer still, with its emphasis on adaptability in terms of process, product, and people. Still missing is an adequate understanding of and solution to the often-destructive power unleashed upon the poor project manager by the unmet expectations of the customer, management, and team.

New mental models (explanations of how people think about things in the real world, what their assumptions are based on) are needed to deal with these real-world people-centric issues that cause so much pain and suffering. For example, Mike Summers, senior HR vice president at Celanese Corporation in Dallas, Texas, has an interesting and successful stakeholder management paradigm that evaluates several key issues, including metrics, rewards, processes, and people, at the beginning of projects and then across time. "Projects occur within these dynamics," Summers says. "Too much focus on the project in an insular fashion can create misalignment, lack of integration, variations elsewhere in the organization, and stakeholder nonsupport."

Triple Expectations Pyramid

As shown in Figure 1-2, on page 17, each face of the Triple Expectations Pyramid encompasses the expectations of your customer, your management, or your team and is itself also a triple constraint triangle, with schedule, cost, and performance (requirement or scope) constraints. *Successfully balancing these nine constraints simultaneously is what makes project managers worth their weight in gold.*

As I said in Chapter 2, simply hitting your technical targets— that is, the schedule, cost, and performance goals that were established early in the project—is *not* the definition of success. I've seen many managers fail to thrive despite the fact that, on paper, they met their goals. Why? They did not successfully balance their technical goals with the expectations of their customer, their management, and their team.

The Expectations of Your Customer

Several statements from project managers highlight the disconnect between customer expectations for performance and the team's desire to do creative work that comes from customer expectations.

These pain points often result in a lot of extra work for everyone involved. I'm sure you have additional pain point examples of your own.

Pain points that come from the customer include:

- *He has unrealistic dates.*
- *She tells my team what to do. How can I drive the team when the customer is directing them?*
- *He backstabs me with my management.*
- *She is always pushing for more features and doesn't want a cost or schedule impact.*

As a project manager, you have to ask yourself why the customer undertakes these actions. The answer is not as simple as "People are illogical." Actually, they aren't illogical. They are almost always very logical, if only you take the time to find out the basis of their logic. If you don't understand why the customer is acting this way, your chances of successfully satisfying that customer will drop, and a great deal of your precious time may be wasted while you try to deal with the ramifications of that lack of knowledge. Let's look at each pain point from a viewpoint that includes the customer's motivations.

> **He has unrealistic dates.** Does he have unrealistic dates because he believes your company sandbagged the schedule or because of a toxic management style in which he pressures you for an aggressive date to ensure that you will make your more conservative date?

> **She tells my team what to do.** How can I drive the team when the customer is directing them? Does she tell your team what to do simply because you let her do so? Or does she think you don't know what you're doing and she has to direct the team for you to ensure her success? Does she do so because of an "I'm paying for this" mentality?

> **He backstabs me with my management.** Does your customer do this in an effort to leverage extra things from your management? Or is he simply just talking with an old friend (your boss) in an effort to ensure success?

► **She is always pushing for more features and doesn't want a cost or schedule impact.** Customers always want more, and often they don't know what they really want when the project starts. You have to determine if the customer is pushing for more in an effort to get something for free or because she is puzzling it out as she goes.

To succeed, you must understand the answers to these questions and come up with solutions that work for everyone. To do so, apply your key set of values, like those shown in Chapter 2. For example, if communication and trust are key values (as they are for me), then explain to the customer that you would like that sort of relationship. Also, throughout the project, use your values as a way to politely question the customer on his or her actions. In this way, you will gain congruence with your customer *through your values*. We discuss the expectations of your customer in detail in Chapter 4.

The Expectations of Your Management

Here are some of the pain points involving supervisors or management that are commonly mentioned by project managers. Let's look at each pain point from a view that includes possible management motivations.

► **He micromanages me.** Maybe your supervisor is just trying to be extra-precise in his efforts to help you. Maybe he doesn't trust you, or perhaps just the contrary, and what you view as micromanagement is simply an overreaction to being ignored by his prior management.

► **She manages upward; she ignores me.** Maybe she has poor people skills and simply doesn't know how to properly mentor or coach you. Perhaps she is truly evil and cares only for herself. Or perhaps she has the sort of personality that prefers to serve those above her rather than leading those below.

► **He wants me not to tell the customer (or upper management) the truth.** Is he being micromanaged? I have seen otherwise nice people act this way when managed in a toxic way. Has a customer in his past who knew too many details about how the sausage was made caused him pain?

➤ **She wants me to know all the minute details.** Does she act this way because she lacks trust, or does she act this way because she was trained to expect that technical managers should know everything that is going on in their organizations? I knew a VP in a design organization who proudly told me he measured his managers on whether they could answer "two questions deep into the details or ten questions deep." Perhaps she is simply not able to realize that different levels of an organization require different management skill sets.

Why, why, why do they act this way? you ask yourself as you ponder these statements and others like them. Then you must find a solution that will work for you. For example, Dr. Barbara von Diether, who was an international consultant for Shipley Associates for twelve years and later a dean and assistant to the president at Utah Valley State College in Orem, Utah, adds this pain point and solution: "If you have a manager who doesn't respond to e-mails requesting resources, or is uninvolved in the project but seems likely to show up later demanding to know why you made certain decisions, be sure to include this last line on every e-mail or memo: 'If you have any suggestions for change to this action, please respond.'" This strategy actually saved Dr. von Diether's job once. After being questioned about several decisions, and after she showed that she had actually asked an upper director for his input on twenty-four memos, Dr. von Diether was told to go clear out her desk and return. When she returned, her supervisor had another job for her. A better one. We discuss expectations of your management further in Chapter 5.

The Expectations of Your Team

Some common team pain points are listed here. Let's look at each pain point from a view that includes possible motivations for your team.

➤ **I'm a manager; they don't respect me.** Are you still trying to be one of the gang? Are you still trying to be a technical expert at one or more of the areas of expertise on your team? Do you fill the proper role of a project manager to lead the team?

▶ **They ignore my direction.** Perhaps your direction is misguided or even wrong. Consider whether your guidance helps team members solve their problems. I guarantee you that if your direction does help them with their issues, they will not ignore you.

▶ **They complain and whine constantly.** Why can't they just work? Are they bad people you should get rid of? That's pretty difficult. Or maybe you just haven't listened to and helped them with their real issues.

▶ **They hide the truth.** This means they don't trust you. Figure out how to win their trust. The best suggestion I have for you is to quit looking at the project from your perspective and instead to look at it from your team's viewpoint. Do that, and trust will blossom.

Again, answer for yourself why your team of outstanding people is doing these things. What do their actions have to do with your actions or inactions? What values are you managing them to? What can you do about all this? We discuss expectations of your team further in Chapter 6.

Putting It All Together

Thriving within the Expectations Pyramid is being able to balance schedule, cost, and performance goals simultaneously with the expectations of your customer, management, and team so that all parties are satisfied with the results.

Per Dr. Von Diether, a real-world example of doing this well comes from the government procurement red team review process. The original Space Station proposal for NASA was bid competitively by two major organizations, McDonnell Douglas and General Dynamics. It was a massive, $14 billion project. McDonnell Douglas assigned 176 engineers and other technical people to the writing team. The company knew that the turn-around time between the release of the Request for Proposal (RFP) and the submission of the proposal would be short, so it assembled the team a year in advance. It hired several former NASA employees to produce a mockup of what the proposal might look like, and then the 176-person team was given two weeks to turn out a proposal based on the mockup.

By going through the entire proposal process, the team and management worked out all the flaws in the flow of work; focused everyone on the win strategy; mitigated any equipment, space, or process problems that arose; and turned out a seven-volume proposal in the required time. When the actual RFP was released, a year later, the McDonnell team was ready to go, and the proposal was released on time and within projected budget. McDonnell got the job from NASA.

Now that you have a basic understanding of the Triple Expectations Pyramid, we get down to the details, with a chapter devoted to each of the three sides of that pyramid. Chapter 4 covers the expectations of your customer, the person who is paying for the endeavor!

CHAPTER 4

The Triple Expectations Pyramid and Your Customer

IN ORDER TO ACHIEVE SUCCESS, you as the project manager must scale all three sides of the Triple Expectations Pyramid. Managing stakeholders' expectations is the first step toward TACTILE Management success, and the most important stakeholder is, of course, the customer. If you can't manage and meet customer expectations, then, no matter how many hours you work, you'll never tame the project management jungle.

As I said in Chapter 3, success means not just meeting the technical goals of a project but also finding the intersection where achievement of technical goals meets stakeholder expectations. Among those stakeholders—the customer, your management, and your team—your customer's expectations take priority, because customer expectations drive all the others.

What is it that customers want? It's not a great mystery. In general, customers want the best product for the lowest cost, they want it on schedule, and they want the features they were promised when they were being offered the moon to sign on the dotted line with your company.

But, once they've put their project in your hands, they've ceded control, and, instead of confidence in your abilities, concerns often take over. Customers are concerned that time is being wasted. If there is a cost-plus arrangement, they worry that you are wasting their money. They want to know that your organization's best and brightest minds are at work on their project, and they want assurances that the organization is properly focused on them and their needs. In addition, a common fear is that they are not being told the full truth; there is the concern that other agendas are at work in the organization. How you put your values to work managing these concerns can dictate whether the concerns dominate the process or the work does.

The customer expectations face of the Triple Expectations Pyramid, shown in Figure 4-1, accentuates performance (scope), schedule, and cost. Determining and understanding how to deal with the expectations of your customer while simultaneously managing technical scope, schedule, and cost issues is difficult. In this chapter, you will find real-life examples of how successfully balancing these sometimes competing priorities can help you thrive.

Customer Expectations: Scope

As mentioned in Chapter 3, the customer often worries that he isn't getting the features that he visualizes. The next story is a twist on that worry and the customer concern that the project manager isn't telling the whole truth.

Tale from the Project Management Jungle: Project X

Marie T. once worked as a program manager for the government electronics portion of a corporation that had several other major business areas, including a semiconductor division. Her project (we'll call it

Figure 4-1: Customer Expectations

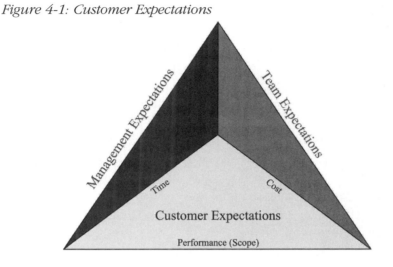

Project X) was to design and build several engineering models of a subsystem within a larger system. As such, Marie T.'s company was a subcontractor to another company (called the prime contractor). To further confuse matters, Marie T.'s company was the prime contractor on a similar competing contract (Project Y), with the prime contractor from her contract a subcontractor on that contract.

As you might imagine in a tangled mess like this, there was little trust. The prime contractor and the government customer on Project X suspected Marie's company of trying to ensure that the project they were prime for would somehow ultimately win out over Project X, so they looked at everything Marie did on Project X with skepticism, making her job quite difficult.

Even though another division of Marie's company designed and built microprocessors, her team had designed an Intel 486 microprocessor (this was a few years ago!) into the engineering models for Project X because the Intel processors were better matches for the overall system requirements. They were all engineers (as was Marie); even Marie had no agenda other than a technical one.

When Intel released the Pentium microprocessor, Marie allowed enthusiastic engineers and interested senior management to talk her into creating a demonstration of the functionality of the system with a new Pentium microprocessor substituted for the approved Intel 486 microprocessor. There were hidden agendas here, possibly among some of the senior engineers and certainly among management, including the desire to show that Marie's company was driving the technical innovation on the contract and within the business area. Without asking the prime contractor or otherwise announcing what had been done, Marie showed the system to a visiting government customer during a planned quarterly visit.

The Pentium was so much better than the 486 (except that it used more power) that it seemed obvious to Marie and her team that a change to the Pentium should be made immediately, and they pushed for that with the government customer during his visit. The government customer then continued on his trip to the prime contractor's site. Of course, when he mentioned the Pentium demonstration, a storm broke out.

Marie knows she should have worked through the chain of command. Her explanation is that they were incredibly busy and that she has always had a blind spot when it comes to asking for permission when the answer seems obvious. Often, that comes across as arrogance; this was one of those times.

Somehow, the Project X prime contractor and the government customer imagined that there was a plot to reopen the debate on the microprocessor choice, and they thought that Marie was perhaps going to try to push her company's processor into the design. Why anyone would imagine that she would choose the Pentium as the way to make that happen is something she still wonders about.

After much blustering, screaming, and hurt feelings on both sides, the design change was made to incorporate the Pentium. The Pentium, of course, won hands down over the 486. From a technical standpoint, it was simply a no-brainer. From the standpoint of whether the customer's expectations on scope were met, it is a different story. Marie did a poor job indeed in that regard.

Let's look at this story first from a TACTILE perspective, then from the Expectations Pyramid point of view.

TACTILE Analysis

Marie T. made a mistake that many inexperienced PMs make. She was unable to place herself properly in the mind of her prime contract customer, one of her key stakeholders. The ability to see the situation from the position of a key stakeholder is key to developing the ability to manage expectations.

▶ **Transparency:** Marie demonstrated a key blocking behavior that is characteristic of many contractual arrangements: almost a complete lack of transparency with her prime contract customer. She believes that the two-contract situation led the management of the two teams to take an approach that lacked real transparency, and the prime contractor program manager created a relationship almost totally lacking in trust, which wasn't her fault. True enough, perhaps, but she did little to change that herself. Instead of taking the situation as a given, she could have worked harder to build common ground with the prime program manager on these kinds of issues.

▶ **Accountability:** Marie does not seem to have understood her role as a subcontractor project manager. Whether she did so deliberately or not, she allowed her company's desire to exhibit technical competency—to show that it really should be the winner in the two-contract competition—to interfere with her job on the contract she supported. She should have stood firm and not yielded to the pressure to do the demo independent of the prime. Her explanation is that "the situation was like the Middle East in terms of how the two companies worked together." Even more reason to be cautious about situations like that with the Pentium.

▶ **Communication:** Marie seemed to have no strategy for communicating clearly with either customer, instead springing a surprise of considerable magnitude on the government customer during a visit, with no agreed-upon agenda. And she completely ignored the prime contract customer, in essence going over his head to the government representative. A simple phone call to her prime contractor program manager, asking for his permission, would have been a good start.

▶ **Trust:** The story demonstrates the effect of lack of trust on the overall team. Clearly, the weirdness of the contractual situation exacerbated the problem. But Marie appears to have thought very little about the issue of trust in relation to her prime contract customer's expectations. She might have been able to establish trust had she invited him to be present for the demonstration and perhaps even allowed him to present the idea to the government representative. An action like this would have cost her nothing but would have paid large dividends.

▶ **Integrity:** Virtually no one involved in this story demonstrates integrity. There may have been a set of values involved in people's actions (win more contracts and thus funding), but those values did not drive the correct solutions. And certainly no one in charge integrated the efforts of all involved toward a common goal. Quite the opposite occurred, as the project was ended well short of its ultimate goal by the government, after a very large expenditure. Ultimately, several years later, another contract was let because the end mission was viewed as important enough to receive continued funding, but with different companies involved.

▶ **Leadership and Execution Results:** Marie clearly exhibited poor leadership skills. She eventually got the short-term execution results she was looking for with the microprocessor choice, but at a high price in terms of wasted emotional energy and overall team cohesiveness.

Expectations Pyramid Analysis

I mentioned earlier that this story is a twist on a standard scope story. Usually the customer is pushing for extra features. In Project X, Marie thought the customer would be overjoyed at the extra feature embodied in a Pentium solution.

Marie was overly focused on technical detail and on the right technical solution, and she forgot that there were other issues involved with the customer and the prime contractor. She also allowed herself to be overpowered by an external management agenda. Additional cost, schedule, and system impacts don't seem to have entered Marie's thinking. Marie was clearly indifferent to the customer expectations here. A few simple actions, such as clearing the presentation with the prime program manager and possibly including him in the meeting, would have gone a long way toward creating a better solution. Managing those expectations is a key job for you as project manager.

Customer Expectations: Cost

As Mac Rawls of Myrtle Beach, South Carolina, who has served in a variety of sales roles, including regional sales manager, says: "Customers simply want what they paid for, when it was promised." The next story relates how a project manager successfully handled not being able to deal with cost and—less important to the customer—schedule expectations.

Tale from the Project Management Jungle: Three-Letter Agency

James, a Phoenix-based project manager, was brought in to manage a development project funded by a three-letter government agency after the contract was awarded. Development work brings high risk. The customer knew this; that is why the contract was a cost-plus-fixed-fee agreement, rather than one with a firm fixed price. (The government customer pays all within-scope costs plus a fixed fee to the contractor in a cost-plus-fixed fee contract, whereas a firm fixed-price contract is for a set amount of money. If the contractor can't complete the work for that cost, too bad, it still must complete the work.)

James was told by his VP to "hit schedule, maintain performance requirements [scope], and, most important, even though this is cost plus, there is no more money. Don't ask." The customer representatives also emphasized this point frequently to him.

James got the message. As a relatively new program manager he was highly motivated and used several creative methods to keep the costs down and to measure progress. But, with several months to go, he could see he was going to run out of money before contract conclusion, and he felt the customer had the right to know immediately. To James, the customer's options were:

➤ It could find more money.
➤ It could cut scope.
➤ It could even cancel the contract.

It was the customer's decision to make. He decided not to hide the information.

James informed his management and called the contract manager at the agency to notify him that the project was going to run out of money. The customer contract manager turned the telephone line blue with his frustration. Within a few days, James found himself in the customer's headquarters building in a major East Coast city.

Picture this: there were at least ten three-letter-agency people at the table. James was the only representative of his corporation. There were *two* account representatives sitting in the back of the conference room—not at the conference table—distancing themselves from the mess, but still there to support their customer.

James started. "We have done everything we can to hit the contractual cost number," he said, and then explained the measures taken to control costs and to manage smartly. This was received with general wary nods from those seated around the room; they had observed some of this in their visits. He then plunged into the abyss: "I'm sorry," he said, "but trends show we are going to run out of money before we finish—"

An explosion of voices interrupted. "Your VP promised. . . . Unacceptable. . . . What about your monthly cost reports. . . . Your company can pay. . . . I am going to take this to . . ." This went on for what seemed like hours, although it was actually only a few minutes.

James waited. When the emotion ran down, he said calmly, "I understand how you feel. I am sorry, but we are going to run out of money. I cannot change that, but there are options. I thought you would want to know now so you could do something about it." They exploded in anger again.

This went on for the rest of the morning. The customer representatives continued to release their not unreasonable frustrations. The money had been hard to find, and they felt they had received assurances that James's company could do the job for the original cost.

James also believes they were testing him for weakness, for any wavering in his story, to see if he as program manager would commit his company to pay for the overrun. After each pause in their venting, James stayed on point: "I am sorry. I do understand how you feel. Here are the data. We are going to run out of money. There are some options. What would you like to do?"

Finally the meeting concluded, and James left the room. The sales representatives patted him on the back as they took him to lunch, where they said, "You did about as well as could be expected. We'll just have to wait and see."

After a few weeks, the agency came up with the requested funding. James finished the contract for the amount requested, to the new budget and schedule. Sometime later, after victory was in sight, he went to his VP and asked for a fresh challenge *and* a new customer. The VP agreed, and James started a new contract as he finished up the former. His career was not hurt by what had transpired. If anything, it prospered as he moved on.

A few days later, James received a phone call from the agency contract manager. "James, we hear a nasty rumor!"

"Yes, Joe, it's true. I am going on to another customer."

"Well, gosh, James. That's disappointing. Was it something we said? Because you're the best project manager we ever had at your company."

James paused for a few seconds, nonplussed. "Wow, Joe. I can't imagine how you treated the bad ones!"

This may sound humorous now, but for James it wasn't funny in the least.

TACTILE Analysis

James succeeded because he confronted a difficult situation using his personal sense of integrity.

▶ **Transparency:** By telling his management and the customer what they needed to hear, James acted in a highly transparent way.

▶ **Accountability:** James took personal accountability by telling the customer all the details as early as known, even though the customer didn't want to hear it. James did so even though he knew the customer would be quite angry; too often, we shy away from needed conversations just because we are afraid of the response. He also placed the accountability for continuing the project where it belonged, with the customer.

▶ **Communication:** James used an excellent communication strategy. Ultimately, he provided what the customer needed (and a lot more) in the approach that he took. He stayed on point with a very simple message.

▶ **Trust:** Telling the truth in this way ultimately increases trust in the overall relationship. This is apparent from the way the customer reacted to James's leaving. The customer would have been much angrier for much longer had James stayed silent until the project ran out of money, which is often what is done. It is always best to tell customers, the management food chain, and your team what they *need* to hear even if they vehemently don't want to hear it at the time. The wisdom is in knowing what they need to hear, when they need to hear it, and how to present the information. Always be ready to offer a handful of options. Keep on point with a simple message (as James did) that can't be confused or construed differently from what you intend.

▶ **Integrity:** James acted with high integrity; ultimately, this is probably what saved him. He did his job, and this was obvious to all.

▶ **Leadership:** James exhibited the ability to step outside the standard contractual behavior of hiding key embarrassing information from the customer until it is too late for them to do other than what is in *your* best interests. His actions required strong leadership as defined within the TACTILE system.

▶ **Execution results:** James generated the desired business result—a finished project that worked as contracted—and he preserved the relationship with the customer.

Expectations Pyramid Analysis

Cost was given huge priority by the customer. James, by exhibiting the TACTILE Management characteristics quite well, was able to sidestep what would have been a disaster had he approached the project as thoughtlessly as Marie T. did on Project X.

Customer Expectations: Schedule

Customers in the high-tech and IT world often feel hopeless about schedule promises. Their options in choosing companies for leading-edge work are frequently limited, and switching from one company to another is often time consuming and expensive. Many organizations, like the company in this story, take on business without a clear process for dealing with the promises that are made to the customer in order to win that business.

Tale from the Project Management Jungle: MIC

Dan S. served as a manager of project managers for a major division of a semiconductor company. Dan's boss had technical (not business) responsibility for all the design projects for the division. He called Dan into his office one day and said, "Go look at the Project Z schedule and see what date they can really make. We are meeting with MIC [Most Important Customer] next week, and I want to know what to tell the staff before the meeting."

Dan found the team the next day already in a schedule review for Project Z. He spent a couple of hours asking questions about the schedule, which showed a certain month as the finish date. He agreed with the team that the date was aggressive but doable. Dan duly reported these facts to his boss.

The next week, Dan was in a review with the division manager and his staff in preparation for the meeting with MIC. When the business area manager (BAM) went through his summary foils on Project Z, the schedule commitment date shown was two months *earlier* than what the project team and Dan had agreed to the previous week. The BAM made no mention of that fact.

Seemingly everyone texts today, but back then (it wasn't *that* long ago) only senior managers had text pagers. Dan started text paging several people—his boss, the engineering project manager, and the assistant project manager who worked for Dan. "This is the wrong date, right? We cannot make it." No one replied, so Dan stood up and said to the division general manager, "This date is not what was agreed to and is too aggressive. We won't make it."

Dan's boss chose this moment to finally reply via text pager: "Sit down. Let the politicians handle this." Dan had not realized these were politicians—he thought the team was there to have a combination technical/business discussion—but he was silent throughout the remainder of the meeting as much discussion ensued. Finally, likely angry with all of them, the division general manager assigned the BAM an action to figure out the correct date, and the meeting was adjourned. Dan was excluded from further meetings, was not involved with the project any further, and finally lost track of Project Z. He ultimately left the company, though not over Project Z.

Dan does not know what date MIC was told the next week. Dan eventually found out that the project went several months beyond even the date agreed to in the team review, much less the more aggressive date.

This wasn't the first time MIC had not been told the whole truth about schedule commitments, and it evidently finally reached its limit and pulled its business, sending all future new part design and sales to a major competitor, which was a huge blow to Dan's former company. Dan also read in the newspaper that his boss and the BAM on Project Z left the corporation unhappily within a few months of that event.

TACTILE Analysis

The staff of the business failed on all aspects of TACTILE Management, so let's focus on Dan's actions.

▶ **Transparency and Accountability:** Dan incorrectly assumed the staff was operating with an approach to transparency and accountability similar to his own. The culture within his company was secretive—data were hoarded, not shared. The staff was more concerned with its own individual issues than with making a good group decision. Dan totally misread this, which obviously contributed to his inefficiency in working with the staff.

▶ **Communication:** Dan did not generate his desired result by standing up in the meeting. Perhaps a better strategy would have been to talk to others outside the meeting.

► **Trust:** There was no trust among the people in the room. They didn't even trust Dan's response. Dan did not read this. Ultimately, of course, the lack of trust between MIC and Dan's company cost the company a lot of business.

► **Integrity:** Dan had a set of strong values that he used to guide his decisions, including the difficult decision to stand up and speak out to a room of his superiors, some of who were quite unhappy with him as a result. But whom did the staff members think they were fooling, and why did they not have the integrity to tell the truth—at least among themselves—and ultimately to the customer? Had there been real integrity—in both senses of the word—among the staff, would the results have been the same? Imagine the likely wonderful results if the division general manager had had a value of integrity within his leadership approach to this staff. Dan's boss and the area business manager might still be working for the company. And perhaps MIC would still be its number one customer.

John Wooden, legendary ex-coach of the UCLA men's basketball team and the man with the most NCAA men's basketball championships, says, in *Coach Wooden's Pyramid of Success Playbook* (Regal Books, 2005): "Integrity is purity of intention . . . a reflection of the heart." The wholeness that integrity implies is key when leading a disparate group of people, particularly with today's geographically dispersed teams.

► **Leadership and Execution Results:** Dan, for all his personal integrity, misread the situation and was unable to be effective. To be a good leader, you should be in touch with your feelings and understand and be able to state your basic value system to all involved *before* you get into the heat of battle.

Expectations Pyramid Analysis

Schedule was critical to Most Important Customer. In the cutting-edge high-tech markets that MIC operates in, a delay of a few months can allow a competitor to come in with products ahead of MIC, costing the company many millions of dollars. Dan's company demonstrated great arrogance in believing it could continue to treat MIC as it did.

Why do companies act like Dan's and continue to avoid facing the issues that prevent them from succeeding? They do not act on a shared critical set of values—they do not see the context in which these values can prove invaluable. I hope this story illustrates to you the cost to Dan, to his boss, to the BAM, and to Dan's company of not having and acting on a key set of values.

All three of these stories demonstrate, both in success and in failure, how keeping customer expectations in the forefront of all decision making can make the difference in project outcomes. Finding a way to balance the customer's expectations with scope, cost, and schedule means you are standing on the pinnacle of the Expectations Pyramid, and you can see success from there. In the next chapter we'll focus on how you must factor in your management's expectations as well if you want to stay on top.

CHAPTER 5

The Triple Expectations Pyramid and Your Management

SO YOU'VE SCALED the Expectations Pyramid. You have identified your customers' expectations and worked to meet their needs, and you have left them satisfied that they are getting their money's worth from your company and your team. These are important accomplishments, and ones that are critical to the success of your project. However, your challenges are just beginning. Customer expectations are only one face of the Triple Expectations Pyramid, and you can't reach the heights you're striving for until you manage *all* your stakeholders' expectations. Remember, you are aiming for the crossroads where the goals of your stakeholders meet the technical needs of your project. You must keep all your goals in sight if you want to thrive.

If your customer, as discussed in Chapter 4, is your most important stakeholder, then management is the stakeholder group whose expectations can make your life the most miserable. After all, management controls your access to future assignments and promotion. The management expectations face of the Triple Expectations Pyramid is shown in Figure 5-1. Many project managers who can master relationships with customers and their teams struggle mightily with their management because this relationship is the most ambiguous and because it is the relationship for which it is most difficult to define success. If you can't manage and meet your management's expectations, then you won't progress.

What does your management food chain want from you? It wants the same things everyone wants. It wants what it asked for, when it asked for it, at the cost it expects. However, the consequences of failure may be even greater for your managers than for you. Your project may be creating the product or service that their business area will depend on for profit and sales for years to come. Therefore, they want your project to meet schedule, to be under budget, and to perform as requested, but they may worry that you won't get it done. Once they have handed you control of the project, they have relatively little influence over your actions and the

Figure 5-1: Management Expectations

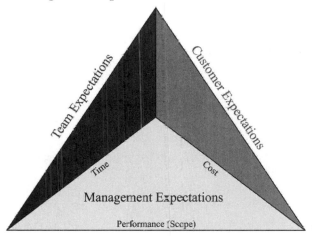

success of the project. Project managers are responsible for the results, but management must also live with those results. Understanding management's viewpoint and what motivates its actions and then building common ground through that understanding will enable you to thrive.

Just as with your customers, you must address issues of scope, schedule, and cost. But, in the case of management, you have other forces to contend with that affect not just your project but also you and your working life.

Two Toxic Management Styles

TACTILE Management is a system that allows you to create a positive people-based culture with your customers, management, and project teams to enable outstanding business results. Learning how to deal with the toxic management styles introduced next is one key to developing this culture, and success here will influence your outcomes with other stakeholders as well.

Managers—themselves caught up in the performance pressures of the modern project management jungle, often ill trained to lead and thus ill equipped to manage their expectations of you—may drift into one of two extremes in management approach:

▶   **Country Club Management:** a lax, undisciplined project environment where project managers are not allowed to build the right culture for success.

▶   **Take the Hill (At Any Cost) Management:** draconian forced-march projects characterized by slavish devotion to one technical constraint (schedule, for example) over all other concerns and intense pressure and scrutiny of every detail by management.

When either of these two toxic management styles—neither of which properly values people—permeates an entire organization, the results can be very difficult for you as a project manager.

Country Club Management

In Country Club Management, project management is viewed as

extra work, as overhead. Management creates this perception (or allows it to happen) because it believes that leaving people alone is the best way to foster creativity. Engineering design and IT organizations that value creativity above all else are often managed this way. Such undisciplined projects are almost always late to schedule in the challenging environment that characterizes so much of today's project management jungle.

Management oversight in these organizations is typically quite hands-off, at least in the early going. Senior managers view their role as a kind of senior professor to the less experienced engineers, providing technical input and guidance even as they themselves get further and further away from the detail. These managers are rarely effective in removing roadblocks for their project managers or in the coaching motivational role. They dismiss those areas as unnecessary soft skills. Getting the most out of you is not fun for them. Often they still want to do your job for you, as opposed to coaching you to success. As mentioned by Duke University's Mike Krzyzewski, the winningest active men's college basketball coach and Executive-in-Residence at the Fuqua School of Business's Center of Leadership and Ethics (COLE), in the product description for his book *Leading with the Heart* (Business Plus, 2001), "Most managers in business rise through the ranks not because of their ability to lead or inspire but because of their knowledge and competence (if not their connections)." As a PM, you will probably react to this management style by feeling irrelevant and unwanted.

Take the Hill (At Any Cost) Management

In Take the Hill (At Any Cost) Management, project management is often wielded as a weapon to beat people into adherence to a work-all-the-time mindset, characterized by statements such as "Whatever it takes. We don't work nine to five, you know. Our people are dedicated—no matter what gets in their way, they suck it up and make it happen." Implicit is that people don't much matter, that they are interchangeable (even if expensive) resources that must be made to do as they are told, and that they can't be trusted.

This management style may make you as a PM feel micromanaged, second guessed, and used. Organizations that are over-ly operations focused may use this management style. Industries characterized by tough margin competition, like the PC industry, and those characterized by a new-product hit-or-miss design cycle, such as the microprocessor design world, may manage this way.

Odd as it may seem at first, both Country Club Management and Take the Hill (At Any Cost) Management are rooted in the same lack of respect for the individual. The first approach is based on the belief that creativity isn't enhanced by people-based project management and the second on a distrust of people that translates into manic energy geared toward driving them to success in spite of themselves. Neither approach realizes that almost all people come to work each day wanting to give their ideas and energy to a successful effort, and, as Coach Krzyzewski says, in *Leading with the Heart*, "Two are better than one if two act as one." Coach K works with only five players at a time on the basketball court. Imagine what fifty or a hundred people can do when they act not as one but as fifty or a hundred acting as one. How about a thou-sand people acting as one? In his book *Microprocessor Design: A Practical Guide from Design Planning to Manufacturing* (McGraw-Hill, 2001), Grant McFarland, an Intel Fellow and senior designer, says that some Intel Corporation projects are that large, and, "for design teams of hundreds of people, the human issues of clear communication, responsibility and organization become just as important as any of the technical issues of design." Sadly, many managers, in my experience, do not understand what is implied in this statement. In the following section, I'll give you an example of how this lack of understanding can play out in the real world with disastrous results, and I'll show you how TACTILE leadership can bring your manager's goals in line with yours.

Your Management's Expectations: Scope

Scope management is most integrally connected to schedule. One cannot discuss scope without the context of schedule impact. Cost frequently takes a backseat in technology or IT projects when it comes to desired new features or capabilities (scope).

Management often knows your customer better than you do, especially if managers themselves were once project managers. They may have even worked with your customers or their organization. They want to maintain their relationships with and look good to those people, and from your perspective they may appear to appease them by promising more than can reasonably be delivered. This leaves you to figure out how to fulfill their lofty promises. Also, they may forget or, in the desire to do well in their new roles, suppress how they felt when their management micromanaged them or made promises about new features to the customer. But don't forget that they are people, too, perhaps more like you than you first realize.

Tale from the Project Management Jungle: Larry's Story

A project manager we'll call Larry once came up to me after a professional society talk. Larry told me how uncomfortable he now felt about the project he had gleefully taken on a few months earlier, after a long stint without a job. 'I came into this ongoing project that was great, with really cool technology. I found out my manager and the sales VP promised the customer extra functionality before I got involved so as to win the business. When I figured that out and made statements that we had to tell the customer we would be late if we added the new functionality, my boss started micromanaging me. He wouldn't let me tell the customer the truth about what was going on. The customer is coming next week from [Far Eastern country] for his first visit since I became the project manager, and he is going to see the truth. Do you have any advice?"

As the conversation continued into the parking lot, I asked questions meant to prompt his thinking. His boss, whom we will call Norman, operated in the shadows, doing everything through one-on-one interactions with Larry. Norman now wanted daily updates from Larry and wanted to approve word-for-word what Larry would say to the customer. He was even taking on a sort of senior designer role, wanting to add and drop features by directing Larry, circumventing the team process. When Larry summoned the courage to mention this, Norman told him he should be flattered that he was getting so much help and attention from someone as experienced and as busy as Norman. Norman had hired Larry, and Larry had no allies in senior management.

Larry felt like he was in a lose-lose situation. He had been spending his family's long-term savings for months before taking the position. He needed the job and couldn't afford to just quit. As an experienced, well-educated project manager, Larry felt deeply disrespected, almost violated by his superior's actions. He also felt that Norman was interfering with his ability to be a good people manager for his team. Finally, being a quietly religious man, Larry was also paying an emotional price, as he felt he was essentially being forced by his supervisor to lie to the customer.

In digital electronics, there are circuit elements called buffers that store information to be used later. I believe that individuals have pain buffers in which they store the kinds of issues Larry was raising. Allowing people to release their pain buffers in a useful way is a skill I feel a manager/leader should have. When Larry seemed to have emptied his pain buffer, I asked, "Anything else?"

Only after waiting for his response, a shake of his head, did I then say, "It's good to know how you feel, but how does Norman feel?"

Larry looked at me oddly, as if that was a question he had never considered. It took a while, but Larry finally decided that Norman (1) wanted things to go well; (2) was trying to help; (3) didn't understand how Larry felt; and (4) might be open to input if it could be presented in a way that seemed helpful in getting things done.

Then I asked, "Anything else?"

I waited impassively for his response. Only when he shook his head did I go on. "Is there going to be an opportunity to speak with Norman about this?"

"We're so busy. I don't see how," Larry replied.

"My advice is to look for that opportunity, that significant emotional event that can be a cathartic moment that opens Norman up to this input. That will allow you two to get somewhere."

Eventually Larry thanked me and drove off into the night.

A couple of weeks later, Larry called me to relay the news that he and Norman had talked after the customer visit. The customer had discovered the company was behind but, instead of blowing up, had rationally requested that the situation be gotten under control and was reviewing closely with Larry a recovery plan that would allow the new scope feature to be added with a small extension to the schedule end date. Turns out the customer had a little schedule margin to play with, and he really liked the extra feature that marketing had pushed into the design through Norman.

Norman wasn't 100 percent convinced of what Larry was saying, but he had agreed to do things differently moving forward. For example, Larry would be the sole contact with the customer; Norman would talk with the customer only during visits. Any phone calls from the customer to Norman would be returned, but with the statement "I will write down your concern and have Larry get back to you on that," geared toward putting Larry in the action position. Norman had agreement from the customer on this approach. The customer just wanted performance. Norman would get fifteen-minute face-to-face status reports from Larry twice per week, and Larry would send interim e-mail synopses of any important events.

"Can it work?" I asked.

"I think it has a chance," Larry replied.

"How do you feel?"

"Much better," he said. "I'm not thinking I'm going to get fired anymore, at least not today!"

"How about Norman? Does he seem more relaxed?"

He paused. "Yes, that would be a good way to describe it."

It seemed everyone had benefited from Larry's willingness to communicate honestly and openly with his boss.

TACTILE Analysis

Larry eventually was able to extricate himself from a bad situation because he connected his actions with his core values and was able to gain at least Norman's cooperation. Overall effectiveness was improved as each man focused on his role.

▶ **Transparency:** Larry's boss was acting about as non-transparently as possible, and he was interfering with Larry's ability to act transparently with his customer and team. Larry took a risk with his action, but there is now at least a chance for success.

▶ **Accountability:** Early on, neither Larry nor Norman was accountable in this story. Larry ultimately found an acceptable way to create mutual accountability between Norman and himself. Sometimes timing is everything.

▶ **Communication:** Larry needed to build the common ground with Norman that would allow him to do his job without constant interference. To get there, he needed to understand Norman better. I do not believe that direct confrontation without some sort of catalyst would have worked. Indeed, research mentioned in *For Your Improvement: A Guide for Development and Coaching,* by Michael M. Lombardo and Robert W. Eichinger (Lominger International, 2006), indicates that direct confrontation doesn't often lead to improved relationships with bad bosses. A better approach is to build common ground and then add to that going forward.

▶ **Trust:** There may never be huge trust between Larry and Norman, but it appears that Larry has started the process toward at least being respected by Norman. Trust between the customer and the team should be improved immensely going forward.

▶ **Integrity:** Larry had to find a way to stop violating his own sense of integrity, to be allowed to tell the customer the truth in the areas that had been left vague or where outright distortion had occurred.

▶ **Leadership:** Larry would never have been able to drive needed culture change within his project; he had ceded control of his job to Norman. His later actions displayed the right kind of leadership to at least give him a chance for success.

▶ **Execution results:** Larry's project would have been an absolute failure if nothing had changed. Now there is a chance for Larry to show his skills, to validate the faith his company put in him by hiring him.

Expectations Pyramid Analysis

By communicating with the customer early about adding scope as it affects the original schedule, Larry and Norman now appear to be working together for the good of all. Hiding that information would have eventually caused someone to play the blame game, likely with bad consequences for Larry, the lowest person in the hierarchy. That would have been a lose-lose situation for all: bad for Norman, the customer, Larry's company, and the project team.

Your Management's Expectations: Schedule

Many organizations keep two sets of schedules for a project. One schedule is shown to the outside world; the other is the schedule that the team is driven to meet. Of course, the due date for the internal schedule is more aggressive, often much more aggressive, than what is shown to the outside world. On the surface, this makes a certain kind of sense: undercommit and overperform. However, management often forgets the choices this drives employees to take, as the following story illustrates.

Tale from the Project Management Jungle: Three-Team Winner

Cheryl, a program manager for a defense electronics firm in the western United States, was assigned a complicated development proposal. The proposal would require expertise from several companies in order to win. She went into the project with several strikes against her success.

First, there was an entrenched incumbent company, which had done a decent job on the prototype design effort. Consequently, Cheryl's company heard about the proposal late in the process and then delayed approving the large expenditure likely needed to win. Thus she was under a great deal of schedule pressure. Also, Cheryl's company was not considered to have much expertise in being a prime contractor or in building competitive teams to take on the big contracts. Finally, it was also considered expensive and was frequently late with its designs.

What she had going for her was the company's strong reputation within the industry for building good technical solutions, as well as for honesty. No one in management at Cheryl's company expected her to win; that was why they had assigned the proposal to her.

Cheryl used her strengths in team building and analysis to craft an effective process of recruiting other contractors for her team. The standard defense-industry approach often views the proposal team-building effort as essentially a way to guarantee percentages of the contract amount and as a political process of gathering subcontractors with needed constituencies in various parts of the government procurement or technical community. Often, the result is that team member companies are given additional tasks in which they have little expertise in order to make sure the company gets its percentage. Frequently, little time is actually spent in ensuring that the various companies involved fit together into a cohesive team.

Cheryl took a different approach. She was aware of the schedule constraint; in fact, that is what made her realize her approach would have to be different to win. She held all the required reviews, but they were streamlined because of the time constraint.

She spent an inordinate amount of time early on with potential partners interviewing potential teammates. At reviews, she received criticism from her management for doing so, playing into her existing fears that management was going to micromanage her, especially given the time constraint. Cheryl made the decision to reveal to her management as little as possible about what she was doing.

She told potential teammates that she wanted a team united toward the goal of winning the contract, emphasizing both what they could expect from her and what she expected from them, noting that her company had not set a percentage target for itself, and adding that she wanted to interview them for their specific expertise. She also emphasized that the partners would have to furnish the right people for the entire seven-week period of the proposal effort—that the proposal team would really be a team, not a collection of experts dropping in for a day here or there.

When the team was assembled, she treated the members all the same, not condescending to or marginalizing the subcontractor representatives. She deliberately receded into the background in a technical sense, allowing the experts furnished by the subcontractor teammates to have their turn in front of the various management reviews and ultimately in front of the procurement review team at the oral team presentation. To the amazement of all, her team won.

TACTILE Analysis

Cheryl combined a great success with a huge miscalculation. Ultimately, her career didn't thrive in this organization because she did not balance all three sides of the expectations pyramid.

▶ **Transparency:** Cheryl wasn't transparent with her management, a mistake many project managers make. However, she was very transparent with the potential partners and her team. It is thus no surprise that she ultimately had a better relationship with her subcontractor team members than she did with her own management.

▶ **Accountability:** A key part of her teamwork strategy was establishing mutual accountability with the subcontractor partners.

▶ **Communication:** Another critical component of her teamwork strategy was establishing open communications with the subcontractor partners. Under time pressure, she did not do the same with her management.

▶ **Trust:** Trust developed within the proposal team and was the biggest reason why the company won the contract, a significant piece of business in a new business area. The selection board commented on the apparent trust within the proposal team as one of the keys to its victory. In contrast, Cheryl did not build trust with her management team.

▶ **Integrity:** Cheryl's approach with the proposal team was one of immense integrity. The team absorbed that into how it worked together.

▶ **Leadership:** Cheryl believed that in order to succeed she needed a culture that was different from her company's standard approach to new proposals, and she created that culture. This belief, along with the time pressure she was under, led her to believe she had to isolate herself and her team from management. She used the schedule pressure as justification.

▶ **Execution Results:** Her team won—and it won in the right way—with everyone involved feeling that the team had accomplished something great. Cheryl describes this as a peak performance moment in her career in terms of the accomplishment itself. But she goes on to say that, after losing the next tough proposal, her management, still perhaps angry about her actions with the winning proposal, made it clear she was no longer wanted in the organization. In many ways, Cheryl seems conflicted and damaged by that time in her career, but she learned some things that proved useful later.

Expectations Pyramid Analysis

Cheryl, rightly or wrongly, made the calculation that her management would not support an approach that it saw as too *touchy-feely.* She capitalized on the fact that the partners were hungry and would likely cooperate. Also, she displayed integrity and her other values to great benefit with her team, but not, obviously, with her management. She did little to build support with her management and peers, and that ultimately led to ineffectiveness and her eventual departure. Note that it wasn't enough that she managed the other two sides of the Expectations Pyramid well: she did exhibit outstanding and innovative team leadership, and her customer loved how integrated her proposal felt and as a result awarded the contract to her team. Without strong performances on all three sides, however, this talented project leader was left wondering what had happened to what she thought was a career peak performance event. If the value system of your management is different from your value system, it is better to find a way to avoid highlighting the difference, while still finding a way to do what you think is right, lest you suffer Cheryl's fate.

Your Management's Expectations: Cost

Management wants a little margin, a little risk buffer. Thus, many organizations keep two sets of cost estimates for a project, much as they do with schedules. One set is shown to the outside world; the other is what the team is driven to meet. Of course, the internal cost estimate is more aggressive—often much more aggressive—than what is shown to the outside world. Like the double set of schedules, there is a surface logic to this: once again, undercommit and overperform. The problem is that this makes you feel like a liar and also makes you feel that management is persecuting you as it tries to get to the truth.

Management, in turn, thinks you are trying to defeat its reasonable desire to establish the correct cost target. That is why, without evidence to the contrary, it will try to slash some set percentage, be it 5 percent, 10 percent, or more, from your budget. Knowing that it is likely to do this, you may add a little something extra here and there and get caught talking out of both sides of your mouth.

This is frustrating for everyone involved. Read on for a different approach that will leave you feeling more honest and will produce better results than you may be used to.

Tale from the Project Management Jungle: Single Entry Schedule-Keeping

This tale concerns my experiences with a microprocessor core design team, The Gang That Could (Finally). Microprocessors enable our modern age, as they are found in virtually any application (e.g., automobiles, computers, and industrial controls, to name just three) where controlled decision making can be turned into an algorithm. A microprocessor core, without getting too techno-geek, is the key building block for the overall microprocessor. This enables a variety of customers to add custom capabilities that differentiate their particular microprocessors from the rest while still using a standard core.

I was brought into the organization after a corporate-wide search for a project manager who would bring an approach that yielded results without using too much unnecessary process. The core our team designed was going into a microprocessor sold by a business unit, which had a management structure separate from ours. To make it even messier, that business unit had a corporate customer that was going to use the microprocessor in a competitive consumer market. Thus, there was a lot of pressure on the managers above us in the food chain.

Because I was new to the semiconductor business and to the culture of the group, I spent most of the first week or so chatting with people, explaining a bit of my philosophy but mostly asking them for their views on the way previous projects had been managed. I used that information to tailor my subsequent approach.

In my first week, I discovered a piece of good luck. The design manager assigned to the project—we'll call him Nitin—was friendly and open and had high emotional intelligence as well as analytical intelligence. Nitin had not been part of my original job interview list, so we had not met before I arrived.

Early on, Nitin and I agreed that we were not going to keep two sets of books, that it was better to tell people the truth as we saw it and refuse to give in to their pressure. In that decision was the calculation that I had credibility based on the corporate search that had brought me there. Also, Nitin was well liked by our management food chain, and he knew it.

Nitin and I did not agree with the schedule date required by our customer. We also refused to start any design work until our schedule and budget were finished. The project labor budget basically came from the task loading of the schedule.

As you can imagine, eventually Nitin and I were called into the offices of our organization's senior management for what were once broadly called "Come to Jesus" meetings. (A more appropriate term for these sessions has not yet become commonplace. Perhaps "Dad—or Mom—Behind the Woodshed" or a variation will catch hold.) These types of meetings typically are meant to shake some sense into the employee so as to prevent some horrible event that no one wants to undertake (like the employee's removal).

First was a review with Bobby R., a design VP who in the past had been responsible for many successful designs. Second was a review with Julius K., the top VP We were careful not to appear arrogant. We started all these conversations with, "We are not trying to be obstinate. While we work out the schedule that everyone can support, we just don't want to start work and take on needless cost."

We were subjected to great scrutiny, but neither Bobby nor Julius had a problem with our approach, and they supported us. I have always felt that you shouldn't live through the impossible, then have them kill you for failure. If they are going to be tempted to kill you, let it come when you are at your strongest. As we will discuss further in this chapter and in Chapter 6, the project ultimately was extremely successful, finishing the exact day that we committed to.

Nitin and I held out for what we thought was right, and ultimately that action was best for all stakeholders. We delivered a realistic schedule that our team could support, a robust product that was ready well before the rest of the microprocessor so that our management team got enormous credit, and a product that worked well ultimately for our customer. We satisfied all three sides of the Expectations Pyramid.

TACTILE Analysis

Nitin and I fortunately had similar value systems and were able to use them to guide our actions through a difficult situation.

▶ **Transparency:** Nitin and I were completely transparent. We explained what our approach was and why we were doing what we were doing, and we always asked for input. Management appreciated our openness. Turns out they were tired of getting beat up by this customer and had been looking for a different approach.

▶ **Accountability:** We held ourselves completely accountable for the results we generated. We were honest enough not to start work early when that violated our sense of how to run the project.

▶ **Communication:** We established good communication with all stakeholders. They didn't always like what they heard, but that shouldn't be your first priority Ultimately, you want them to be happy with the results, but they cannot dictate how you get there. That is why they hired you in the first place!

▶ **Trust:** Because it was clear we weren't hiding anything, trust went sky high. Management trusted us because we were open to its input. Again, not always liking what he heard, the customer nevertheless trusted that what he was hearing was true.

▶ **Integrity:** We showed high integrity in our honest and open approach.

▶ **Leadership:** This is an example of the right kind of leadership. You are not required to go along with scope, schedule, or cost goals from management or anyone that don't make sense. Of course, you disagree at your own peril. You have to be right!

▶ **Execution Results:** We felt a certain amount of pressure after these events, because we were on the line. But aren't you always? And in this case we were doing things right from our point of view. I'll take that situation any day over, say, Larry's, as described earlier in this chapter.

Expectations Pyramid Analysis

Once management saw that we had done our homework, it did not push for two sets of books, on either cost or schedule. Once management sees that it can trust you, its risk-avoidance behavior, such as asking for two sets of books, goes away. Subsequent requests for resources were much better received from our management, as well. A better overall relationship ensued.

Succeeding in the project management jungle is a feat that requires you to balance seemingly endless and contradictory priorities and to get disparate factions with sometimes competing agendas to focus on one goal—*the team's overriding goal*. But perhaps the trickiest task of all is managing your management's expectations so that you do not just find success in one project but build a career. Keeping the TACTILE values at the forefront of your decision making will ensure that you manage your stakeholders' expectations and thrive in the process.

You've addressed your customers' and your management's expectations, but you're not done yet. You still have to manage your team—and the team can make or break you, as we'll see in Chapter 6.

The Triple Expectations Pyramid and Your Team

MEETING AND EXCEEDING THE EXPECTATIONS of your teams—helping them win—is the best way for you to generate positive business results for your organization. That's where the results are created, after all (see Figure 6-1).

What's required? Many people think a take-charge attitude is best, that you have to tell people what to do. Not me. I find that today's worker prefers as much autonomy as possible within a structure, a framework—we might even dare to say a *process*, albeit one that is as simple as possible. Your job is to match that framework to your team and the work it is doing.

Figure 6-1: Team Expectations

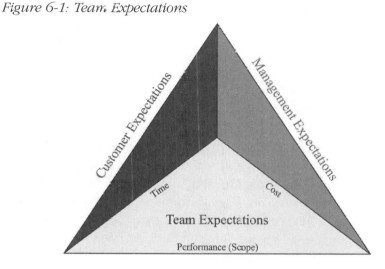

In that spirit, what is it your team expects of you? Simply, it expects you to:

➤ Listen to team members in the areas that matter to them.
➤ Help them to meet their own work goals.
➤ Lead them in the effort to establish and meet the overriding team goal.

Of course, doing these things will make your management and customers happy, as well. Then all your stakeholders' expectations will finally merge into one path that leads straight to the apex of the Expectations Pyramid.

The following stories are personal. I have left myself in them because leading teams is the most personal part of being a project manager, and I want you to feel my experience as closely as it can be communicated.

Your Team's Expectations: Scope

Scope is a touchy subject with your team members. They often assume that you and management will let the scope increase in order to satisfy the customer, causing the team to do extra, unplanned work. The following story turns that assumption on its ear.

Tale from the Project Management Jungle: The Wood-Sorting Yard

I worked as a co-op student for four semesters at a paper mill in my home state of South Carolina while in engineering school at Clemson University. *Co-op* is short for cooperative education, in which a student alternates semesters at school with real-world experience.

This wasn't just any paper mill that I worked in. At the time, it had the widest Fourdrinier in the world. The Fourdrinier is the basis for most modern papermaking. It accomplishes all the steps needed to transform a source of wood pulp into a final paper product. These machines run very fast and are very wide, generating huge economies of scale.

But my first task was not with the sexy Fourdrinier. Rather, it was to design the new control panel for a totally different part of the paper mill, the wood-sorting yard.

I was a nineteen-year-old college sophomore. I had finished three semesters of college, only one of which had included engineering classes. I had never flown in an airplane. I knew next to nothing about paper mills. I certainly did not know how to design a new control panel for the wood-sorting yard.

The wood-sorting yard is the front end of a paper mill, the area where the logs are sorted by size, quality, and whatever other criteria are used. The logs are dumped in the top of a collection of conveyor belts, and then it looks like—if you were a fly on one of the logs—the log ride at an amusement park, except that these are real logs that would easily crush you if you somehow fell into the sluices.

So, how to get the information—the scope or performance criteria—I needed to design the new control panel? I started by finding the sorting operator. Sorting operators in wood-sorting yards have a tough job. Imagine sitting for eight hours per day, five days per week, in a noisy, scary, wet environment, with headphones on to prevent deafness, constantly hitting buttons to sort logs all day, only occasionally getting up to use huge gaffe hooks to untangle jammed logs.

The sorting operator, Darrell, acted like he didn't see me, but eventually he motioned me into the quiet room just off the sorting floor. He glared at me, clearly not impressed.

"I'm here to design your new control panel," I started hopefully.

"Uh huh," Darrell said, his initial impression clearly unchanged.

I showed him the plans from the engineering files. "This is the current drawing."

He glared down at the drawing. "That ain't righhht," he drawled.

"Oh."

In the most dismissive and derisive tone possible, Darrell said, "Follow me,' and he went back out to the floor. He picked up a broom.

Darrell stood in front of a rusty control panel that was clearly in need of replacement. The panel was several feet across, with one hundred or so buttons. "I have to take this here broom and start the thing like this." He used the broom with his right arm to simulate pushing a button far from where he was pushing other buttons with his left arm. "That's what the last college boy left me," Darrell said with another glare. "He dint have the fust idea how to design anything anybody could use."

Somehow I had enough sense to say, "Well, how would you like it designed?"

"What?" Darrell yelled crossly.

"Why don't you tell me what you want it to look like," I said.

His response was a snort, a long glare, and a jerk of his head back toward the quiet room. I followed him, and we started designing his control panel. After a couple more sessions, it was done. A few weeks later, Darrell had a brand-new stainless steel control panel. His broom went back to being used for sweeping.

TACTILE Analysis

This is an example of a young person who had the right instincts and enough sense to follow those instincts but who would not have articulated that well at the time. Realize you may be in a similar situation and let your instincts guide you.

➤ **Transparency:** I was totally transparent with Darrell. I hadn't *learned* how to be any other way.

➤ **Accountability:** By asking Darrell for his input, I demonstrated my accountability and held Darrell accountable for the results. I doubt he complained about "that college boy" again.

➤ **Communication:** Again, I didn't know any other way to act. My open, direct approach inadvertently disarmed Darrell.

➤ **Trust:** Trust, however unlikely, came because of the approach taken on the first three characteristics.

➤ **Integrity:** Try as he might, Darrell couldn't see any reason to not cooperate. Darrell saw a wet-behind-the-ears young kid he didn't like, but my personal integrity came through. And he evidently did want a properly designed control panel.

➤ **Leadership:** This is an example of creating the good local culture needed to solve the issue at hand.

➤ **Execution Results:** The desired results were achieved: a functional new control panel was designed that had the scope needed, and it was done by gathering information from the informed team member, at the same time paying dividends on his motivation.

Expectations Pyramid Analysis

Darrell almost surely had low expectations of me coming into our encounter. By taking the seemingly simple approach of asking for his input and by giving him some control over the outcome, I inadvertently hit on just the right way to overcome Darrell's expectations bias. I also met and even exceeded his needs in terms of scope—not the scope that an engineering student thought he needed, but what Darrell actually needed to better perform his job.

The rest of this chapter concerns my experiences with the microprocessor core design team The Gang That Could (Finally), first mentioned in Chapter 5. A microprocessor core is the key building block for the overall microprocessor; it enables a variety of customers to add custom capabilities that differentiate their particular microprocessors while still allowing them to use a standard core.

The team of very talented engineers I worked with had previously never had a successful project in terms of meeting scope, schedule, and cost, which to them had always been someone else's concern. To them, success had been designing great microprocessors, without the discipline good project management can bring. They were very inwardly focused. Their view of success did not include enabling the success of other stakeholders. Many technical teams, without leadership, view the world in this simplistic way. Quite often, this hinders the dissemination of the technology they create, exactly the opposite of what they would like to see.

The next three stories are really just facets of one larger story. I will provide only one TACTILE Analysis and Expectations Pyramid Analysis, at the end of the third story.

Tale from the Project Management Jungle: The Gang That Could (Finally)—Scope

Because I was new to the semiconductor business, my first task was getting to know people I did this by explaining my philosophy and seeking out their views on the way previous projects had been managed.

As described in Chapter 5, I was met with good luck in the form of the design manager assigned to the project, Nitin, who was friendly and open and who had high emotional as well as analytical intelligence. In addition, while disheartened and overworked in an effort to finish the previous project, the team was at least willing to talk with me. One of the more vocal team members, Sandra, called me out in a meeting.

"You PM guys always promise the customer whatever he asks for; then we are here trying to do it 24/7 and get beat up when we fall short."

Several team members pounded me in this way. I didn't take it personally. Instead, I listened and tried to understand the world they lived in every day.

Eventually, Nitin and I found ourselves in the office of our internal customer (the microprocessor project manager), Elliot.

After handshakes, Elliot took twenty minutes to talk us through a short PowerPoint document that covered what looked like high-level basic requirements for the microprocessor cores for which we were responsible. Due dates were also shown. He asked if we had any questions.

I had a couple. "Can I look at the requirement document, see how many open areas there are?"

Elliot glanced at Nitin, who nodded as if he knew what was coming. Elliot smiled slightly at me. "You all develop the details for your work, not us."

I see. How convenient. I then asked, "How did you arrive at those dates?"

Elliot smiled and said, "Don't worry about that. These are your dates. Okay?"

Not okay, but we shook hands again and left. Nitin and I went back to the design center. Remembering Sandra's admonishment, I said, "You know the tasks, the team, the work better than anyone. Right?"

Nitin nodded.

"Are there holes in the requirements document, things we have no idea how we are going to get done?"

Nitin smirked a bit. "Sure."

"Considering that, can we make those dates?"

Nitin shook his head. "I doubt it."

"I thought so," I replied. "So we're in trouble?"

"No more than normal," Nitin said.

"Would you like my advice?"

He nodded.

"You will never be stronger than you are now at the beginning of the project. Right?"

Nitin nodded.

"Why live through the impossible and then have them kill you?"

"Yeah?" he said.

"Why don't we figure out what scope we can deliver by the end date Elliot is demanding and commit only to that date/scope combination?"

Nitin smiled. "Tell me more."

We talked off and on for several days, then went to the team leaders with an idea to work with them to analyze the open scope items and to create a milestone schedule with enough detail (a milestone every two weeks) that it would allow us to convince ourselves and others that we weren't sandbagging—that is, trying to pad the schedule. The team somewhat skeptically agreed.

Your Team's Expectations: Schedule

As mentioned in Chapter 5, many organizations keep two sets of schedules for a project. The internal, aggressive one is what the team is driven to. Of course, the team knows that the other schedule exists. This immediately creates a trust barrier. Team members assume that if you will lie about that, you will lie about other things. Your team resents being managed this way, and it underperforms when managed this way. Read on for a different approach.

Tale from the Project Management Jungle: The Gang That Could (Finally)—Schedule

"Elliot, we can't commit to any other date," Nitin said. "This is our date."

Elliot shook his head at us as if we were deranged. "Unacceptable," he said. "I, or more likely my boss, will be talking with Bobby and Julius." Bobby and Julius were the senior VPs for the design center we worked in.

Elliot's reaction was not unexpected. The date we came up with was later than his required date by a couple of months. Our date was based on reasonable assumptions about the existing scope and the unresolved scope items, made by people who were actually going to do the work. We did not (as many people assumed) sandbag the dates. The end date was still quite aggressive.

Nitin and I developed a multistep approach. The next step was a kickoff meeting with the team leaders. We told them what Nitin and I expected of ourselves—how we intended to help them remove roadblocks—and what we expected of them.

For the detailed schedule, we told them that each of them was going to create, update, and ultimately own his or her sub-schedule, which fed into the unified team schedule. Their schedules should show the name of the one person assigned to each task (no multitasking), with tasks lasting no longer than two weeks.

We told them we were going to have weekly team meetings that emphasized team problem solving, not status reporting, and encouraged them to come to the meeting prepared to bring up and solve problems. We showed them the one-page form we wanted them to fill out and bring to each team meeting. They were skeptical, but less so now that our stance on the end date had not resulted in our removal. As word filtered through the building that management and the customer were not rejecting our approach, Nitin and I began to see more positive energy from the team. This only increased as we hit one milestone after another.

Your Team's Expectations: Cost

It is axiomatic that costs always increase on a development project anytime they are re-estimated. Cost is what your team represents to anyone looking at your budget. The team knows that many project managers will assume that the easiest way to lower cost is to get each team member to work more hours. Seems like basic math, right? But this approach demoralizes the team as it chases the proverbial carrot that the project leader seems to hold out of reach. The team will assume that of *you* unless you find another way to generate the needed business results.

Tale from the Project Management Jungle: The Gang That Could (Finally)—Cost

As previously mentioned, we held weekly team meetings with the task leaders, with each task leader bringing his or her own one-page report to the meetings. The information in these reports was all that we allowed to be discussed in the team meetings.

One input we asked for was unforeseen new tasks. We hoped that, armed with this information early, we could forestall the adding of a huge number of new designers (read: cost) throughout the project.

Designers are precise people who want to do everything right. This is a great attribute, unless you define the word *right* in terms of perfection. I prefer excellence to perfection. In lieu of any other way of analyzing situations, engineers and engineering managers will almost always err in the direction of more, not less. More tests, more tasks, more, more, more. All this, of course, adds cost and delay to the project.

Task leaders frequently ask to add new tasks to the schedule. This almost always means the addition of more people (cost) to the project, because every individual contributor's time is almost always fully (or more) planned. In response, I started asking a series of questions. First of all, I never questioned whether the task needed to be done or acted as if I were a technical expert. I only asked what the impact of doing that task would be: to the nearest milestone, to other team leader's tasks, or, occasionally, to the end date. I asked the questions in such a way as to stimulate discussion among the team leaders. As a result, most of the required new tasks went away, and, if the new task really had to be done, we generally developed a way to work around any added delay.

I took this approach because I wanted to teach the team leaders how to get out of their cubicles and work together, but it also served to keep costs down and to prevent impacts to the schedule. None of the business types ever complained to me about cost. Schedule was critical, scope was important, and cost was actually the least important of those three criteria on our microprocessor core development project.

What were the results? Simply fantastic:

➤ We never missed one of our milestones.
➤ We hit our two schedules on the days we'd committed to.
➤ Our design center VP was congratulated for the success in Julius's staff meeting.
➤ Nitin and I went on to promotions and bigger assignments.
➤ The process we put in place enabled the team to tape out five more cores on time, long after we were gone.

TACTILE Analysis

Some of the managers involved still use these approaches on current projects in the various companies they work for. This demonstrates the business results—ongoing for years—that are possible when the right values are applied effectively.

▶ **Transparency:** We were totally transparent—not only with our team but also with everyone else. For example, we kept only one set of schedule books. The initial list of milestones we came up with in conjunction with the team leaders never shifted. We told our customer, our management, and the team the same final commitment date, and it never shifted. The team knew everything we told management.

▶ **Accountability:** All the team members knew what was expected of them and what they could expect of others. Accountability went all the way to the design center VP, who himself told the team in a kickoff meeting that he was there to help if needed. Later, when he actually did so, the team's morale soared. By creating an accountability culture, Nitin and I dealt with a tendency to vagueness that many people use to create plausible deniability. Vagueness in dates, vagueness in requirements, vagueness in many things is how some people (deliberately or otherwise) place you on the hook.

▶ **Communication:** We worked hard to create an environment where the right information got to where it was needed as quickly as possible.

▶ **Trust:** Trust bloomed in this environment. People began to enjoy their jobs and working with their teammates. One senior designer told me, "Finally, I can sleep at night." Another said, "So this is how this project management stuff is supposed to work."

▶ **Integrity:** The team members got to the point where they just believed whatever Nitin and I told them. The customer and our management did also. Everyone was able to relax in that environment.

▶ **Leadership:** We created the desired culture change.

► **Execution Results:** The results were as good as anyone could have ever expected—and took less actual work than the team was used to.

Expectations Pyramid Analysis

By creating a TACTILE environment, we were able to exceed our team's expectations. The team worked hard, but, more important, they worked smart. They were able to achieve work/life balance and still meet the corporate goals. Our management was quite happy with us, as was our corporate customer.

Using the Triple Expectations Pyramid

In Chapter 3, the Expectations Pyramid was used as a graphical illustration to show that the expectations of your customer, management, and team—the three key stakeholder groups—are critical. Expectations management requires that you determine the desires, wants, and needs of your three key stakeholder groups— your customer, your management, and your team—so that you can craft a solution that leaves them all satisfied with you and your project's results. The R.101 case study in Chapter 3 showed how to summarize the expectations of the three stakeholder groups. This chapter and the preceding two illustrated the concepts by focusing on one stakeholder group per chapter.

But how can you integrate all this into a successful project? First, your chance of success will be higher if you pick the proper project. For that, you need what I call a *black box project*. A black box project has clear inputs (requirements) and outcomes (deliverables and dates) that you advertise, but inside the box you are allowed to implement your approach without interference. What kind of projects are the best candidates? Important projects, like the microprocessor cores discussed in this chapter, where management was open to change because of past lack of success. This point was made to me in the Q&A phase of a talk I gave, and that person was absolutely right.

What would constitute an improper project? These are projects where management or the team leaders are sure they are already correct, where nothing will get them to agree to change.

Once you have the right project, evaluate it using the Expectations Pyramid format. Let's use The Gang That Could (Finally) as an example.

▶ **Customer Expectations:** TGTC was a microprocessor core for another internal corporate customer. This customer used our core in a microprocessor that it in turn sold to an internal customer in a completely different part of the same large corporation. Their customer sold the ultimate product into a very competitive consumer marketplace. The ultimate customer had a bad history with my new organization, as did our internal local customer. Elliot, our internal customer, was the program manager for the microprocessor unit. He expected a continuation of the poor schedule performance from earlier projects. Elliot had no real concern for our costs, as they were not directly billable to any cost account he managed. He expected to be able to keep the requirements liquid and vague so that they could be changed at the direction of his customer or as his engineers figured out certain approaches. Both sets of customers—Elliot and his corporate-level customer—acted on their worries about poor performance by trying to dictate dates to us that had considerable management reserve built into them and by trying to micromanage us.

▶ **Management Expectations:** From the time the project was approved, my management chain felt tremendous heat to perform for this corporate mega-project. That is one reason it conducted a corporate search that ultimately wound up with me as project manager. It expected a difficult project and worried that a failure might destroy careers. It also worried that the destroyed careers might be theirs.

▶ **Team Expectations:** From previous experience, the team members expected a chaotically managed project, characterized by unreasonable dates, fluid requirements, and heavy pressure from management. They also expected project management to be a non-value-added waste of time and extra work. Nitin and I decided from the beginning to tailor the approach to the team members and to tell them that good project management wasn't *extra* work; it *was* the work. As their worries failed to materialize into reality, increasingly the team began to cooperate with what we were doing, and our approach eventually became the project culture.

▶   **Results:** TGTC finished ("taped out," in the semiconductor design world) to the day that we'd committed to, amid great fanfare and happiness. Nitin and I were ultimately promoted, as were some in our management chain. No one lost his or her job.

Next, choose your personal approach on the basis of a set of characteristics by which to manage. Use my TACTILE list, or modify it as you see fit. The key point is that you need a connected philosophy by which to lead. Otherwise, you will get lost when the going gets tough. Remember Larry's sad fate, recounted in Chapter 4.

In Chapter 2, we talked about soft and hard skills. In an effort to combine the two, I defined strong skills as *the ability to use any robust process—like Lean, Agile, or Six Sigma—combined with the ability to get results through people.* Take a look at your strong skills. Seek input from others on your effectiveness, and fix what you think needs fixing.

Before actually implementing this approach on your own project, take some time to reflect on what might go wrong and create plans with your team for how to deal with these eventualities. Chapters 7–11 examine the five key phases of a project—Initiating; Planning; Executing; Monitoring, Controlling, *and* Reporting (as mentioned in the Introduction, reporting is a key addition for me); and Closing, from the perspective of several pitfalls you may encounter on your way to success.

PART IV:
Avoiding Pitfalls in the Five Key Phases of a Project

CHAPTER 7

Initiating

INITIATING (OR INITIATION) BEGINS at the point in which a specific project, one of the many potential projects an organization may be considering, is approved. When a new project is initiated, these questions are key:

► Who will lead it (PM assignment)?
► Why is this project being done (project charter)?
► What will be done (project scope)?

Obviously, you want to be assigned to projects that will enhance your career. In many organizations, a complicated political process is involved in determining which projects get approved and then who gets assigned to the key roles on those projects. This process is certainly not always logical and straightforward.

Make sure you know *why* you accept each new project assignment. There are valid reasons why you might not. For example, Bea twice passed up the chance to work on promising projects in her organization, once because she didn't trust the senior management to support her in what she could see would be a tough situation and once because she wanted to give a promising subordinate a chance to run a project. Refuse too many projects, however, and you may quickly find yourself outside your organization's mainstream or even out the door.

Also, be aware that organizations often misunderstand the project charter process during initiation, allowing other agendas to piggyback onto it. They also pay too little attention early on to the details of the project scope. The key areas in initiation are:

► PM assignment
► Project charter
► Project scope

PM Assignment

Being assigned to the right projects is critically important for your career; therefore, much of this chapter focuses on PM assignment. Just how *are* project managers assigned for major projects? Bob Carroll graduated from Harvard University in 1972 and has an extensive background in manufacturing management and project management. He has written numerous papers on technology issues, lean manufacturing, and self-directed work groups. Carroll has hired many project leaders in his career in a variety of roles, including operations section manager at Motorola, Inc., in Scottsdale, Arizona. His list of desired qualities for strong project leaders includes the following:

► Solid engineering/science education
► Intelligent
► Honest/trustworthy
► Strong people skills
► Self-confident
► Self-starter

➤ Positive attitude

➤ Open to new ideas and new ways of doing things

➤ Loyal, nonpolitical

Mark Finger, HR VP at National Instruments (NI), says: "The best engineers often don't make the best supervisors." Finger also mentions that NI spends a great deal of time identifying and matching needed skills with potential leaders. It looks for the ability to communicate effectively so as to bridge the various stakeholder viewpoints, to manage and balance risk, to have the willingness to make the tough calls (even if unpopular), and to do all this in a way that is consistent with NI's values.

So, if you have the leadership qualities your supervisors are looking for, can you count on getting the plum assignment? Certainly, this will get you on the short list. After that, organizational factors are involved. In my experience, these organizational factors are (in no particular order) as follows:

➤ Availability of desired individuals

➤ Organizational politics

➤ Recent past performance

➤ Grooming considerations for career growth

➤ Diversity

➤ The number of new projects requiring a project manager

No wonder getting things done and generating business results is so hard, considering how few of these factors are directly related to getting the product out the door.

Two pitfalls commonly occur with PM assignment, and they can have lasting negative effects on both the future success of the project and your success with it.

Project Pitfall: Project Manager Assigned After Project Approval

Often, there are more potential projects than there are seasoned project managers. Consequently, before the project receives final approval, the organization may assign someone to oversee the project who will not be the execution project manager. This task may be only one among many other tasks for this person. She may not even be a professional project manager; for example, she may be the marketing professional who is pushing for the project. She may not make the time or have the expertise to ensure that the necessary actions are performed, leaving a mess for the next project manager. Sure, the right checklists will be filled in and the required reviews will be held, but the effort might not match what is required for the project to have the highest chance of success.

You might think: *How can I be held accountable for issues that predate me back to initiation?* Larry, the project manager in Chapter 5 who took what looked like an interesting project assignment after months of unemployment, made a statement much like that to me. Larry seemed to meet all the criteria for a strong project leader, but he struggled for a long time because of issues that had come up before his involvement.

There are several things you can do before you accept a position to ensure that the position will work well for you. First, to deal with what are admittedly complicated and confusing situations wrought with emotion and overwhelming time and financial pressures, you need a set of bedrock beliefs, established before trouble started, upon which you will base your decisions. My bedrock beliefs are embodied in the seven characteristics of TACTILE Management. They drive my actions at work and, increasingly, in the rest of my life. Take the time to think about what your key beliefs are and how you would deal with situations like Larry's.

In addition, you must decide before the next project what your personal approach will be concerning issues not of your making. My advice is to identify and give voice to such issues early, before they attach themselves to you. Include a page of discovered issues/risks in your first and all subsequent monthly ops reviews. Refuse to lie to customers, management, or your team. It might be better for you to find a new job, no matter how painful that might be, than to try to find your way through the minefield of other people's problems. Your values should drive how you live and work. If trust and other similar values are important to you, you will not find playing loose with the truth a viable strategy.

Next, you must network. Technical people often prefer working technical issues by themselves rather than building personal networks. To avoid Larry's fate, you must get out of your cubicle and network often to meet people who share your values. Develop a key set of friends who watch out for one another. One technical person who does this well is my Texas Aggie friend Ann. Ann used her very extensive Central Texas network of not just co-workers but also college classmates and professors, neighbors in affluent West Austin, fellow choir members, Scout parents, soccer parents, and several other groups, developed and nurtured over many years, to find an entirely new career field that she loves and in which she is successful.

Finally, improve your emotional intelligence so that you can better discern situations that don't work well for you. IQ is the traditional measure of cognitive abilities. In contrast, emotional intelligence (EQ), per Reuven Bar-On, creator of the Emotional Quotient Inventory, as quoted by authors Marcia Hughes and James Bradford Terrell in *The Emotionally Intelligent Team* (Jossey-Bass, 2007), is "a cross-section of interrelated emotional and social competencies, skills, and facilitators that determine how effectively we understand and express ourselves, understand others and relate with them, and cope with daily demands." This sounds to me like the definition of a good project manager. If you accept this definition, it seems fair to say that many of us technically trained folks have higher IQs than EQs.

Actions You Can Take

To improve your EQ, assign yourself the following action items:

▶ Read Daniel Goleman's *Emotional Intelligence: Why It Can Matter More Than IQ*, a classic. Also, Dr. Reldan Nadler's *The Leader's Playbook* is a hands-on guide to using emotional intelligence concepts in the business world.

▶ Take an EQ assessment from a professional. Bar-On's EQI, Hayes Group's Emotional Competency Instrument, or the Mayer-Salovey-Caruso Emotional Intelligence Test (MSCEIT) will give you insight into yourself and your situation. The easiest way to find a qualified professional to administer these assessments is through the International Coaching Federation (ICF). There are chapters in most major cities. Also, the companies that own these assessments can give you a list of qualified administrators.

The Skinner and the Three Letter Agency

Some organizations use two different individuals in planning projects. I call one a *trapper*, used to win a contract or gain approval of a project, and the second a *skinner*, used to run the project. The use of different individuals for these two roles allows for organizational plausible deniability, a kind of collective shrugging of the shoulders over who is really responsible when things go wrong. Was it a bad contract or just poor execution by that young, or new, or inexperienced project manager? Project managers in these situations can easily become scapegoats if something goes wrong and they have not had time to build a strong network of support.

James's Three Letter Agency, mentioned in Chapter 4, is just such a story. When you are the skinner, wondering if you are set up to fail, you may feel like giving up and going wherever the organization culture seems to push you. But it is always best to tell customers, your management, and your team what they *need* to hear, even if they vehemently do not want to hear it at the time. The wisdom (or emotional intelligence) is in knowing what they *need* to hear, when they need to hear it, and how to present the information. Be able to present a handful of options. Keep on point with a simple message that cannot be confused or construed differently from the way you intend.

Telling the truth in this way will ultimately increase trust in the overall relationship. The Three Letter Agency customer would have been much angrier for much longer had James stayed silent (which is often what is done) until he ran out of money and then told the agency.

Be aware when you are in a skinner position. Decide if the risk is worth the potential return. For James, everything worked out, but this is certainly not always the case.

Project Pitfall: PM Assigned Before Project Approval

Let's move on to the position of the project leader who negotiated the contract or led the team through the company's internal project approval process. This position may seem better because you have more knowledge and control, but it can still be dangerous, because stakeholders are tempted to say, "You should have thought of that during the preapproval phase; it is in your baseline." Or if the requirements (scope) document is vague, they will be certain that whatever issue you raise was already addressed and will likely say, in angry, dismissive terms, something like, "I am sure that was covered during the project approval process. Why are you bringing it up now?"

Actions You Can Take

Here are a few steps you can take during initiation and then build on as the project moves through the other phases:

▶ Focus on closing all the unresolved actions you can before the approval meeting through discussions with stakeholders or others who can resolve the issue.

▶ Document the approved baseline as best you can, along with the open actions, action owners, and due dates.

▶ Publish this baseline list of actions, and make sure some part of your ongoing monthly operations review package discusses any actions that are still open each month. You don't have to overdo this; one page will likely be enough to keep those important needed actions on the awareness burner.

▶ Drive the remaining actions quickly to closure as the project proceeds.

Tool You Can Use: The Interpersonal Situation Awareness Tool

Many of us may think we can handle any assignment given. In some cases, we may think we have no choice about whether to accept an assignment. The Interpersonal Situation Awareness Tool (ISAT), shown in Figure 7-1, provides you with some self-generat-

Figure 7-1: Interpersonal Situation Analysis Tool

	Situation Analyzed: Pegasus Rider Name: Doug Russell						SUM
	FIVE KEY QUESTIONS	1	2	3	4	5	
A. Relationship w/key project partner							0
B. Relationship w/your supervisor							0
C. Relationship w/your customer							0
D. Your personal power in situation		X 2 =					0
E. Relationship w/your team		X 2 =					0
F. Net relationship w/supervisor's key peers			X 3 =				0
G. Net relationship w/other key stakeholders			X 3 =				0
						TOTAL	0

ed information to raise your awareness when you must decide not only which projects to take on but also which relationships will require some effort.

Situation awareness (SA) means ensuring that the necessary information to make a decision is available and understood by the decision maker. The ISAT is meant to give you situational awareness on a key decision: which project assignments you will agree to. The seven ISAT components are:

1. Relationship with your key project partner (A)
2. Relationship with your supervisor (B)
3. Relationship with your customer (C)

4. Your personal power in the situation (D)
5. Relationship with your team (E)
6. Net relationship with your supervisor's key peers (F)
7. Net relationship with other key stakeholders (G)

In the pages that follow, we're going to go through each of these seven components one at a time. As you fill out the ISAT, be brutally honest with yourself. This is a learning exercise, geared to help you better understand yourself, those around you, and the situations you are in so that you make wiser choices in the projects you choose to work on.

Five Key Questions

The sections in the ISAT concerning the relationships with your key project partner (A), supervisor (B), and customer (C) use some or all of the five questions that follow. On a scale of 1 to 5, with 1 = not at all; 2 = somewhat untrue; 3 = neutral; 4 = somewhat true; 5 = extremely true, answer the following questions, as applicable to sections A, B, and C. The "he" or "she" mentioned in the questions refers to your key partner, supervisor, or customer, depending on the applicable section. (Note that Questions 3 and 4 are not scored for your customer relationship [section C].)

1. To what extent is she committed to your success?
2. To what extent does his basic value system around people management and concepts like integrity, transparency, accountability, communication, and trust match yours?
3. To what extent is she supportive of you in the organization, especially when things get tough?
4. To what extent does he seek to understand and maximize your personal strengths?
5. To what extent does she apply what you consider useful emotional intelligence to your benefit?

These elements, by no means based on a statistically valid survey (but several technical professionals did fill out versions of the questionnaire to help me calibrate it), are what I have found to be predictive of several positive outcomes on projects I have worked on:

- ▶ Maximization of personal strengths
- ▶ Potential for corporate profitable results
- ▶ Potential for personal high reward and recognition
- ▶ Relative degree of my happiness

Some of the questions may be difficult to answer before you get to know the people referenced in each section. It is imperative that you develop the empathy skills to be able to quickly read the people around you, particularly the key individuals cited in the following discussion. Don't be afraid to seek information from and about these individuals in interviews or discussions via the organizational grapevine.

Seven Key Relationships

Let's look at each of the seven key relationships covered in the ISAT.

1. Relationship with Your Key Project Partner (A)

This person is Sancho Panza to your Don Quixote, your closest partner on the project. (Or he may be Don Quixote and you are Sancho Panza. I hope you get the point.) You decide who fills this role; there is no set description for this person, except that you both have the key roles in the project's success. Your input on your key project partner can be summarized with the following formula:

$$(A) = (Q1 + Q2 + Q3 + Q4 + Q5) = \underline{\quad}$$

2. Relationship with Your Supervisor (B)

Your input on your relationship with your supervisor can be determined with a similar calculation:

$$(B) = (Q1 + Q2 + Q3 + Q4 + Q5) = \underline{\quad}$$

3. Relationship with Your Key Customer (C)

Your relationship with your key customer (the person at the

organization who is paying for the project, not the person who will use the product) can be tough, because you spend less time with your customer than you do with your key project partner and supervisor.

If possible, go see your customer in person and get to know him or her before the contract or project is approved.

Your input on your relationship with your customer can be quantified with this formula:

$$(C) = (Q1 + Q2 + Q5) = \underline{\quad\quad}$$

4. **Your Personal Power within the Organization (D)**

The underlying question here is: *to what extent is the organization desperate for your skill set?* This score is so important that it gets double points on your overall ISAT scorecard.

Is the organization smug and complacent about its past performance? If so, score this question 1. If the organization is desperate for new ideas, score 5 here. Your personal power score is calculated by the following equation:

$$(D) = \underline{\quad\quad} \times 2 = \underline{\quad\quad}$$

5. **Relationship with Your Team (E)**

Your relationship with your team, as in your personal power section (D), is so important that it gets double points on your ISAT. Is it chomping at the bit for the approach you want to use? If so, assign a score of 5 here. Is it complacent about how things have been done and strongly resistant to anything new? If so, assign a score of 1.

Have no idea because you are new? During your initial interviews with key project personnel, you should gather information to help you form an opinion. Mention some of your planned approach and see how the team reacts.

Your team evaluation score is calculated as follows:

$$(E) = \underline{\quad\quad} \times 2 = \underline{\quad\quad}$$

6.   **Net relationship with Your Supervisor's Peer Group (F)**

How we as project managers handle the interaction with our management after an assignment is given is something few PMs consider. Your approach going in is key to future success. Do you view management as allies who can help or as irritations to be humored?

Evaluate the key members of your management food chain. They are considered key if they are somehow involved in your project from a management perspective and can affect your current or future positions. Then subtract the number of people in the chain who are demonstrably negative about you from those who are demonstrably positive. Enter this net number in the ISAT spreadsheet.

I often have had great allies in management or among the HR people who supported the organizations I was in. Conversely, I have had occasionally found my way obstructed by influential managers, usually managers who felt that my project management function was gaining too much influence over how their people were directed.

Your relationship with the management food chain can be calculated with this equation:

$$(F) = 3 \text{ X (net } \textit{positive} \text{ people minus } \textit{negative} \text{ people)} = \underline{\quad}$$

Note: The maximum you should enter here is plus or minus six.

7.   **Net relationship with other key stakeholders (G)**

Occasionally, other individuals peripherally connected to your project are so good or bad for you that they bear including. For example, on a major government project I was involved in, two technical experts (not the customer—he was an army colonel in another state) who worked for the contracting entity were so negative about my company that they significantly affected our ability to do many things, including some of the high-performance team-building activities that we wanted to accomplish. On the other side of the equation, we were fortunate on the same contract to have a high-performance team expert from industry assigned to our team. Subtract the negative people from positive ones, multiply the net remaining number by 3, and enter the result:

Other score (G) = 3 X (net positive people minus net negative people) =

Note: The maximum you should enter here is plus or minus six.

Now, total $A + B + C + D + E + F + G$. This is your ISAT score for the subject project. The most valuable information comes from comparing pre-project and post-project scores.

The ISAT is not meant to give you the right answer; it is just a tool to help you evaluate key aspects of the situation. Had I performed an ISAT on various projects throughout my career, I believe I would have endured a good deal less stress, possibly choosing to not take on some of those projects. At a minimum, I would have done things differently *during* the projects.

The ISAT can help you in many ways. Obviously, you can use it in the initiating phase to convince yourself to avoid or accept a project. During planning, you can also use the output of the ISAT to identify key people problems so that you solve them early, before they cause major problems that result in the usual firefighting or diving catches required by lack of planning.

Of course, the higher the score, the better, but the total score is not as important as how you use it. Understand your weak areas, and find ways to improve or neutralize them. But, more important, maximize your strengths. To do this, assign yourself a series of actions to drive the needed change. An accountability buddy, someone to whom you can report your actions and progress, is a good idea, also.

Project Charter

The project charter documents the goals and objectives of a project in relation to the organization's overall business strategy (which, we hope, is informed by an intimate understanding of the customer's needs), as well as some high-level information on the investment required. John Berra, chairman of Emerson Process Group, mentions that Emerson connects projects selected to the overall business strategy through its New Product Development (NPD) process. Its approach builds successful organizational consensus through the inclusion of representatives from a broad cross-section of involved functions into what he describes as "Wrestlemania," where open discussion of ideas occurs in a dynamic manner.

The project charter is a key part of the *D phase*—for "define"—in DMAIC, a basic process in the Six Sigma methodology. You should use your project charter as a way to rally everyone involved behind a common goal, but also be aware that project charters can be misused in ways that hamper your efforts to lead a successful project.

Project Pitfall: Misuse of the Project Charter: "Let's Jump on *This* Train"

Juan, a marketing manager in a major semiconductor company, described to me the outline of a great new product aimed specifically at the consumer marketplace. As you might expect, this marketplace requires quick reaction and short cycle times. Juan was also serving as the default project manager, not a role in which he had much interest or experience.

Juan did not know what to do about a particular issue that emerged. Members of senior management, in an effort to spread the initial investment across more business units, were using the project charter process to broaden the design to fit more applications. His fear was that this might cause his company to miss what appeared to be a golden consumer opportunity.

Management's hijacking of your project charter—jumping onto and disrupting your neatly structured and organized project train, then jumping off when it gets where it wants to be—can ultimately cause you to fail as you miss your narrow market window or have a defocused project scope.

Actions You Can Take

These steps can help you avoid being derailed by a hijacked agenda:

➤   Point out the opportunity cost to the product in such delay. This will display communication skill.

➤   Have a one-on-one with each decision maker in an effort to change the tide, which should build trust.

➤   Find a sponsor in a key organization to support your fight. Again, trust is emphasized.

➤   Stand firm and refuse to commit to the same final schedule dates with the increased scope, thus displaying your integrity.

Project Pitfall: Dangerous Assumptions at Greasy Grass Creek

There is another point around the project charter to discuss. *The PMBOK Guide* says, "Initial assumptions and constraints will also be documented. This information is ultimately captured in the Project Charter.' The dangerous word here is *assumptions*.

A U.S. army general, a project manager of sorts, accepted a potentially dangerous but relatively common assignment during the Indian Wars of the late 1800s. His project was to clean out a group of Indian warriors who had gathered at what the Indians called Greasy Grass Creek. This general, one of the most distinguished of his time, suffered a devastating and completely unexpected defeat. Why?

His defeat occurred because of several incorrect initial assumptions he made as he approached the project. These concerned:

➤   The number of warriors facing him
➤   The warrior's relative desire to fight
➤   The supporting resources (reinforcements) that would be necessary

The name of this general, as you may have guessed, was George A. Custer. In addition to these incorrect assumptions, Custer made his first order to attack without having accurate information on the village's size or location. In that way, key project constraints were seriously understated. Custer also refused new tools (Gatling guns) that would, almost assuredly, have helped him achieve his objectives. Finally, he refused extra human resources from the Second Cavalry on the mistaken belief that his Seventh Cavalry could handle anything.

There is a fair amount of evidence that Custer was not the bungler that some historians portray. In fact, Custer had a distinguished history of service during the Civil War, including devising the strategy that led to the pinning down of Confederate general Robert E. Lee immediately before Lee's surrender at Appomattox Courthouse. But no project manager who hopes to thrive can make that many erroneous assumptions as he comes into project planning and execution. Of course, Custer certainly did not thrive. His fate was much worse than that!

Actions You Can Take

In organizations without a common culture of high integrity, people don't believe the information they receive, and stakeholders assume all sorts of things (usually bad) about your work output. Don't let bad assumptions disrupt your plan. Instead, take action:

▶ Root out bad assumptions early by asking probing questions, and then deal immediately with what they uncover.

▶ A common initial management assumption is that you padded your estimates to make your job easier. To remove this perceived pad, various stakeholders will push for more features, more scope, more of everything, making it virtually impossible for the project to succeed. You cannot accept behavior like this without telling them the likely result. Be known as someone who tells the truth, no matter how irritating the truth may be.

▶ By communicating transparently how your dates were determined and what the results will be if the schedule is arbitrarily pulled in, you can put TACTILE Management techniques into useful action.

Project Scope

A project's detailed technical requirements are frequently captured in what is called a scope document. The purpose of the scope document is to detail the customer's needs, rather than how the team will accomplish its goals. The pitfall here is not so much what is written as what is *not* written—that which is left TBD.

Project Pitfall: The To-Be-Feared TBD

TBD, which of course stands for "to be determined," may look innocuous there in your scope document, but it presents a clear and present danger for you as a project manager. Those three letters represent a four-letter word to you: *risk*. They enable vagueness, a condition that may have dire consequences for you later when budgets or schedules affected by those TBDs aren't met. Compound that situation by not informing your customer or management up front of the impact of these issues, and your goose will likely be cooked when the truth finally comes out.

It is true that I have never seen a scope document that was totally finished during the initiating portion of a development project. Often, they are not 100 percent finished even during the project's execution. But you accept a huge risk (to project *and* career) if management mandates a conclusion date for the project while ignoring significant open scope issues (TBDs)—all of which are conveniently forgotten later—and then insists on holding the team to the mandated date, even though the impact of the now-determined TBDs is finally (in horror) understood.

Arun A., our post-silicon test manager, explains the problem with requirements documents as a translation issue across different levels of abstraction and detail. "Typically, there is a high-level requirements document from marketing that gets translated to a product level requirements document." Small portions of this requirements document are given to various members of the design team, "who have to parse out what this really means given the available technologies in order to decide how to design the circuit." There are often multiple ways to do so. "They document their approach in a micro-level document. My job is to ensure that enough discussion occurs between the right people to make sure that the 'green elephant' described in the requirements document doesn't somehow turn into a 'white elephant' in implementation."

The skill in all this is the ability to first determine what is truly significant. Experience helps in this regard, but you can't know everything. You must build good working relationships with key individuals on the team who can help you look out for the things you don't know well; there are well-intentioned people all around you just waiting to help if you ask in the right way. For example, I once had a test manager who made me look good for years. His price? Frequent conversations in which I mostly listened to his litany of problems and how he resourcefully solved them.

Once you understand your highest-risk open scope areas, then assign them to the right people for action and make sure they have the time and focus to resolve the issue. Then focus on these actions until they are closed.

Some stakeholders may have a tendency to wave away any remaining gaps in the scope document: "That will be worked out later," or "This is a high-level document only, and that detail is in the noise." Often project managers feel intimidated by these people. Big mistake. They may hang you later for problems that arise. Bottom line: you shouldn't allow your project out of initiating and into formal planning without a clear understanding of the TBDs in your requirements document. These TBDs represent open scope that is a risk, and you must estimate the potential costs or schedule impacts of these risks. And make sure management knows that this information is documented for communication to the organization. Ensuring that intense sunlight is cast on the right information is one of the best ways to guarantee that mold and decay do not set in and that the right actions are taken.

"This is unrealistic," some of you will say. "We can't make that work. Management won't play fair—they'll ignore all the open issues and drive us to their impossible date no matter what we do." Like you, I am not a miracle worker. I have tried the approach described here on impossible people, and it did not work. But it has worked much more often than it has failed.

Actions You Can Take

Here are some ideas for combating the dreaded TBDs:

▶ To close TBDs, schedule periodic reviews with the scope document owners to keep them focused on closing open scope issues.

▶ Also, highlight open TBDs in your monthly operations reviews or other reports to management.

Preplanning the Plan

Some organizations simply do not understand the essential difference between the process of approving projects (initiating) and the subsequent planning and executing of these projects. Data that are completely acceptable for the purpose of approving a project may be—if left unchanged—woefully inadequate for planning and execution. As you get closer to the actual work itself, you will need more detail. A sort of detail gap can be created if this is not understood. Arun A. works for an organization that understands this and that has a process that telescopes down into deeper detail at appropriate times on the project timeline. To deal with situations where this is not the case, you need to preplan the plan.

This means you need to view the project holistically and with the long view in mind. Know that actions you take (or don't take) now will have consequences later. Specifically, you should:

▶ Ensure that the key project documents that come from initiation, such as the scope document, preliminary budget, list of risks, and schedule, are examined from the perspective of the team's execution for gaps that will impede planning.

▶ Identify actions needed to close those gaps, and drive them to closure in a way that builds the team's cohesiveness.

▶ Focus with laser-like intensity on closing the open actions before you start the planning process. Refuse to officially start planning until a strong effort is made to close those gaps.

▶ Identify when it is time to stop this and move on, but move into planning only with a list of actions that clearly shows what needs to be done and identifies the risk in doing so.

▶ Start the process now of being transparent, holding yourself and others accountable, and driving clear communication and trust with integrity, while being the right kind of strong leader to enable the team to generate the desired execution results.

Avoiding Toxic Management in Initiation

In Chapter 5, we discussed two toxic management styles: *Country Club Management*, a lax, undisciplined project environment where project managers are not empowered to build the right culture for success, and *Take the Hill (At Any Cost) Management*, a draconian forced-march project environment characterized by slavish devotion to one criterion only (for example, schedule) to the detriment of all else and intense pressure and scrutiny of every detail by management. This book's major goal is to show you an easier way to manage through people while still generating the desired results for your organization. The bullet points in the preceding section will help you create the right culture in initiation, but what specifically can you do to ensure that neither toxic management style creeps into your project during this crucial phase?

To combat Country Club Management:

▶ Don't take the job if management won't support your approach. If it is happy with the same-old same-old, you won't succeed.

▶ Make sure your project management approach fits the team's maturity and culture. Don't push team members too far. There is a delicate balance.

▶ Create and enforce the rule that the team will not start the effort early in some sort of misguided desire to make progress. In Country Club Management, the idea is operative, that you should "just get started, we'll work all that out later."

To combat Take the Hill (At Any Cost) Management:

▶ Don't give in to the panic and fear of failure that causes much of this type of management behavior. Trust in yourself, and build a trusting team.

▶ Question why extra metrics and/or an extremely detailed schedule project management process might be overkill and unnecessarily cost the business money. Often, organizations do these together, but sometimes they do one in isolation from the other.

Share papers and studies that show that efficiency in knowledge worker teams is complex and requires more than just demanding that they do "whatever it takes." For a start, read Susan Lucia Annunzio's *Contagious Success*, first mentioned in Chapter 2.

Case Study: The Path Less Taken

This ongoing case study will compare TACTILE concepts to a typical approach through each of the five phases of a project called Alpha Omega, inside the communications division of a hypothetical tech company called Best Technology Company (BTC).

PM Assignment

The communications division staff of BTC needs to assign a project leader to its key project, Alpha Omega. The decision is a critical one; the last few key products from the division have been late. BTC is still viewed as a leading tech company, but Mark Simpson, the division general manager, has been told in no uncertain terms that his job rides on getting Alpha Omega out on time.

Standard Approach: "Of Course It's Ravi"
Division Staff Meeting, Pre-Project

"Okay, everyone quiet down, let's try to finish. We'll shelve the team training for us then. There is little interest, and just no time," says Mark Simpson, the division general manager. "Last item: assigning a PM for Project Alpha Omega. Frankly, this has taken too long already. We need to decide today. I had hoped Deborah would join us, but our CTO is evidently too busy elsewhere."

Groans from around the table. The meeting is already thirty minutes late. Several people start typing on their portable assistants.

Simpson continues. "So, we've got it down to two candidates—"

A slender, intense figure interrupts him. Sebastian Turner, the division VP of engineering, says, "I'm sorry, Mark, what's to decide?

Why would it be anyone but Ravi? He is the best young technical mind we have. Knows how we do things. Good education, right work ethic, and he pulled us out of the fire on Orion Catcher last year. It's his time."

"Ravi is not a leader," chimes in Delores Grant, director of HR. "He tries to micromanage everything, doesn't communicate well, Sebastian. You know the corporate initiatives this year—"

"And this new person—Sheila Jackson—she isn't even really an engineer," Sebastian counters, a slight note of scorn in his voice.

T.J. Anderson, head of marketing for the division, speaks up. "She understands the customer, she does have an engineering degree from a fine school, along with an MBA from Stanford, and a lot of experience getting teams to be successful. In this business, that isn't easy. Look how she helped Sanders Turner on its last chip for the printer market. Word on my grapevine is that ST was dead until she got there."

"Not technical."

"She is technical enough."

"My people won't respect someone like Sheila," Sebastian replies flatly, almost coldly. "Her education and experience are fine, I guess. She is certainly likable, I'll grant you. And an African American woman would be a great coup for HR, I'll also grant you. But surely we shouldn't hire her just because of those things. Engineering isn't comfortable with an outsider running this project. My goose is cooked if we miss this one. *All* our jobs are on the line with this one."

And that's the bottom line. Delores and T.J. fight on for a few minutes, but there is no support from the rest of the room. Finally, Mark says, "We are a tech company, after all, folks." He glances at T.J. and Delores. "I can talk to you two for a while if you want to talk, but we're going with Ravi."

TACTILE Approach: "A Surprising Way of Choosing"
Division Staff Meeting, Pre-Project

Mark Simpson, the division general manager, stands to get everyone's attention. "Last agenda item," he says. "And I note we are still on time." He pauses.

There is general laughter. He continues. "We need to finish the decision on the project leader for Project Alpha Omega. I had hoped Deborah Tabor would be here. We could use input from our CTO, but never mind. As we all agreed at the beginning of this process, we are going to have one person summarize the pros and cons for the candidates. Since Engineering is going to have to live with this hire, Sebastian is going to be that person. Before he comes up here, I want to thank him for being open to a different way of working together."

. Sebastian smiles slightly as he comes forward. "It was mostly Delores. I just started listening to her."

"That is true," Delores says to general laughter. Then she smiles. "You all deserve the credit. It's not easy to learn to work together in a different way, but you're doing it. But we all know this wouldn't be working without Mark's sponsoring the process."

"Sponsoring is the kindest word for what Mark did," Sebastian says with a smile, reaching the front of the room. "But I agree; the process has worked. Here are Ravi's pros and cons." He projects the list they had all been e-mailed a few days earlier. He then shows a list of Sheila's pros and cons.

"As you can see I have incorporated your inputs. Thank you all for that. Are there any comments?"

They talk for twenty minutes or so, with everyone in the room speaking at one time or another. People are passionate but civil. The room does not break down into two positional groups.

When there seems to be no more comments, Sebastian says, "Is that it, then?" When they nod, he speaks. "I have to admit that I would feel better with Ravi. He knows so much, has been here long enough to know our ways. He is a great guy and has gotten us out of a bunch of scrapes. But these past few years have been so hard. There has to be a better way. Maybe Sheila is the way to go."

And that's what they do.

Project Charter

As discussed earlier in this chapter, the project charter states what the project is going to accomplish. Involving the team appropriately in the process of clearly defining the problem they are going to work on is the right thing to do. Organizations often don't do so, because they think it unnecessarily takes too much time or makes this harder and more complicated than it needs to be. As you will see, Ravi and Sheila both view the project charter as important but approach the generation of it differently.

Standard Approach

Project Year 0, Two Weeks In
Key Managers Team Meeting

Ravi can see that his project staff is ready to leave. "Getting close; just a couple of things left to talk about. First, we need to finish the project charter."

Bennett (never Ben) Lee, the lead circuit designer, reacts. "We need to get back to work, Ravi. I've got four designers to check on who just started on the ASCRAM logic. This management junk is NVA."

Jiao Lee, the design assurance manager, nods. "I agree. No value in this."

Mira Bose, his post-silicon test manager, says, "Ravi, why do we not just use the charter that was approved by the project gate approval committee?"

"Yes, well. You know how it works around here. The marketing people have some new features to add, and they want them in the charter so that they can make sure we add them."

The room erupts in anger, with several people cursing.

Here we go again, Ravi thinks.

TACTILE Approach

Project Year 0, Three Weeks In
Division Marketing VP T.J. Anderson's Office

"Sheila," T.J. says with a slight edge in her voice.

"T.J.," Sheila replies with a slight smile.

"I was instrumental in getting you in here. I am very glad you are running the project, but this is how we do things here. Wireless SHDMI is absolutely required for Alpha Omega. The charter needs to say it, so it will get done."

"What about the schedule approved by the gate committee?

What about the scope document? You are on the committee. How can you just change it now?"

"Things have changed in the marketplace Gotta add it. We are afraid OMC (Our Major Competitor) may have it on its next chip."

"T.J.," Sheila says, still smiling, but less than before.

"Sheila," T.J. says flatly.

"I will be glad to give you a schedule/cost impact for adding the new feature, if the division gate approval committee asks. It will take the team a week after that to do the analysis. Until then we proceed with the charter as defined. I will put SHDMI on the must-have list for the first revision."

"This is too much process BS. This is not how it works in the real world," T.J. mutters as she leaves Sheila's cubicle.

"It is real in my world," Sheila replies to T.J.'s departing back. "Has worked for me many times. See you later." She goes back to the e-mail she had been preparing. The issue never comes up again. Sheila adds SHDMI to the "must-have" features list for the next revision.

Project Scope

Organizations have different ways of dealing with the open items in their scope documents. While it is true these documents are never finished—they do continue to evolve somewhat over time— there is more than one way of dealing with the situation.

Standard Approach

Same Meeting

They are still venting. Even Jiao Lee appears upset—and Ravi has never seen Jiao upset before.

Ravi tries to reassert himself. "This is what happens every project. You know we have to stay current with marketing. We have one last thing to cover. Everyone *be quiet!*" Finally, they calm down. They're good people; they know the score.

Ravi continues. "On the open items in the scope document— here is a list. I have assigned each of you the appropriate open items. Let's go through them one at a time."

Bennett (never Ben) Lee glances at the document. "But there are fifty-eight items on here, Ravi. We'll be here all day! I've got other stuff going on."

Ravi doesn't even look up. "This is the only way these things ever get closed, Bennett. Now, let's get started."

Two hours later the meeting ends, unfinished. They have discussed only twelve of the open items and closed only five of them. Ravi has scheduled another two-hour meeting for the next day.

Another day shot, they drift back to their cubicles. Jiao calls her day care provider to plead for a few extra minutes beyond their strict 6 P.M. deadline. Bennett (never Ben) walks quickly down to his designers' desks. He doesn't care; he has no one to go home to, anyway. Zev Cohen, the verification manager, calls his wife, Sarah, to inform her when he will be home. She tells him she understands and will keep the kids ready for their bedtime story until he gets there.

TACTILE Approach

Project Year 0, Two Weeks Later
Division Operations Review

"That's right, Mark," Sheila says brightly. "We have closed all but three of the fifty-eight TBDs we had in the scope document coming out of division gate approval. A couple of new ones came up."

"This is great news, Sheila," Mark replies. "Why was it so easy? Normally, isn't this a huge issue?"

Sheila smiles. "Well, I didn't say it was easy. But we just focused on this as a team."

T.J. pipes in. "You must have burned a lot of team BTUs doing this, huh?"

Sheila turns to Sebastian. "What are your people in Engineering telling you?"

Sebastian looks up from behind his keyboard. "They are telling me that this is all you've had them doing, so they've been able to focus and get it done. No one has staffed up their teams at all. There's no pre-work going on."

Sheila nods. "That's right. After all, we are still in pre-planning. Even though initiation was approved when you all gave the gate approval, we can't start planning until we know what to plan. Getting the TBDs in the scope document closed will take us a long way toward that."

Grudgingly, the people in the room look at Sheila with new-found respect.

Seeing this, division GM Mark Simpson says, "Can't argue with the results! Never seen a project this clear at this point."

No one argues with him.

TACTILE Analysis

There is no indication in the standard section that the staff is working to any sort of process, while in contrast in the TACTILE section it is clear that the staff is working closely together on a team approach.

▶ **Transparency:** In the standard section, the staff just argues from individual positions that have little organizational cohesion. In contrast, it is clear in the TACTILE case that division general manager Mark Simpson is driving a team process that is transparent: everyone involved knows what is going on, and there are no agendas other than running the business.

Ravi, in the standard section, allows himself to be caught by the forces that swirl around him. He is just going about his job, without overtly trying to create a successful culture. The idea of transparency seems irrelevant to him. In the second (TACTILE) example, Sheila is transparent in all her actions.

▶ **Accountability:** In the first (standard) PM selection story, the team members do not hold each other accountable for statements or actions, while in the TACTILE example they clearly hold themselves more accountable.

Sheila holds her team, herself, and her management accountable. Ravi thinks he is doing so by holding long meetings on the open items, but he isn't allowing them to do their jobs; he is attempting to micro-manage.

▶ **Communication:** The standard PM selection team drops quickly into two positional camps. The TACTILE team employs a decision-making process that minimizes positional argument, allowing the discussion to turn into a team decision.

Ravi is task oriented. Sheila has a much larger, more holistic view. This translates into Ravi's team grumbling as he applies the whip; by the end of Sheila's sections, we see her team and management beginning to understand why Sheila's approach is a good one. Sheila is clear and direct. Ravi only appears to be that way.

▶ **Trust:** The first PM selection team members do not trust one another. This is because they have not been transparent, held each other accountable, or used a clear communication approach. By contrast, the members in the second example do have trust.

Ravi's team is shown in what is a very typical nontrusting environment on modern project management teams. Many people say, "That's just the way it is" and dismiss the view that the team members don't trust anyone—not Ravi, not management, not really one another. On the other hand, you can see the trust beginning to grow with Sheila's team.

▶ **Integrity:** In the TACTILE example, the leader of the team, general manager Mark Simpson, is shown to have demonstrated integrity by putting a process in place that works. This allows the team members to relax and follow his example; it brings the best out in them. In the standard case, he is much more passive. The team members, essentially left rudderless, act like him. It isn't surprising when, out of frustration, they break into positional camps.

Ravi is a fine person and a hard worker. He is just caught in a toxic culture without a way to make things happen, so he tries to bull his way through. Sheila, by following her sense of integrity, is beginning to establish her desired culture.

▶ **Leadership:** Simpson does little to provide a culture in which the team can work well together in the standard example. In the TACTILE case, he does provide leadership by creating a framework within which his team can work and by taking the right actions when they are needed to drive change. That team works much better together.

Sheila's team and management are responding to her. Ravi is

struggling to exert himself with his team, even though he was chosen because of his technical expertise and his long service within BTC.

▶ **Execution Results:** The division management team makes completely opposite decisions on team leadership. Only time will tell which decision will turn out to be more effective for the business.

Sheila is planting the seeds of eventual success. Ravi, on the other hand, is simply reacting to each situation as it occurs. His approach is just to work hard and tell people what they need to do.

The initiating phase of a project is often given little attention or is ignored outright, a situation I've always found incomprehensible. While it is true that initiating stands alone more than any other phase or process group, you can almost guarantee failure from the start if you do not get certain areas right.

For the initiating phase, focus on these areas:

▶ Get on the right projects, and, if you didn't do so, figure out what to do about the situations you do find yourself in. The ISAT tool can help you find ways to succeed even if you land on the wrong project.
▶ Pay close attention to how the scope document is being managed.
▶ Use the project charter process to help create the proper project culture.

Got these areas right? Then you're ready to move on to planning.

CHAPTER 8

Planning

THE PLANNING PHASE DEFINES how a project is to be done. *The PMBOK Guide* suggests that the best way to accomplish this is through the creation of a project management plan, with a section that covers each of the following nine knowledge groups:

1. Scope management
2. Time management
3. Cost management
4. Risk management
5. Quality management
6. Human resources management
7. Communications management
8. Procurement management

9.   Integration management

Many project managers make the mistake of creating project management plans that are simply pasted together subplans from the nine knowledge areas. Instead, you should view planning as a part of an integrative and holistic system composed of the five interconnected phases of a project, as shown in Figure 8-1. While initiating is part of the system, the thought construct of an integrated system really becomes important in planning. The five phases are shown separated by information band gaps and connected by project culture. The project culture can be thought of as a viscous medium, with greater or lesser friction and opaqueness that are based on how well you create a culture that is transparent, creates communication, and implements the other TACTILE characteristics. The information band gaps are a way of showing that you (because you are responsible for the project culture) must create a culture that allows ideas to flow and communication to occur easily across these unseen but real barriers.

I have been involved many times in lengthy planning efforts, some of them taking several months. Only on the most complex, such as the $6 billion Iridium satellite communication system, did the size and scope of the project truly warrant such effort. After

Figure 8-1: Modern Project Phase Interconnections

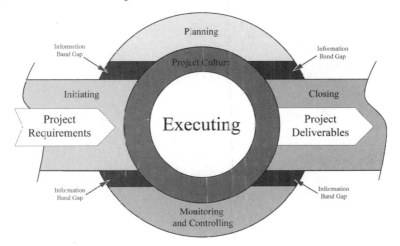

observing much wasted effort over my career, I eventually developed a simpler way to use whatever scheduling, risk management, and budgeting tools were required by the organization. Doing so is one key to what this book is all about.

Planning well is only the start of your success. Too often, organizations think that, once a plan is approved, success will just be a matter of working blindly according to the plan. And if that doesn't work, they often blame you, the project manager. Or they think planning is unnecessary. To use a sports analogy, a good project plan is like a good game plan; it is only an effort to use the talent available to maximize the chance of success. There is no guarantee of victory!

Planning means deciding how your project is going to be managed for the duration of the project through three frameworks:

➤ Creating the initial (baseline) plan
➤ Discovering and addressing new information until final plan approval
➤ Flexibly looking ahead

Creating the Initial (Baseline) Plan

When you start the process of creating the initial or baseline plan, beware of three project pitfalls that can undermine all your hard work and set you up for failure before you really begin:

➤ Underplanning: All Thrust, No Direction
➤ Overplanning the McClellan Way: DO-Loop to Infinity
➤ Agenda Hijack

Project Pitfall: Underplanning: All Thrust, No Direction

Particularly in IT and development, there are many project managers who rush to execute a project without sufficient planning—or even *any* real planning—perhaps because they have had prior bad experiences with overly complicated processes. People around the U.S. space program use a phrase that captures this type of management: "all thrust, no direction." These managers drive themselves and their teams to put forth enormous energy, but the energy is not focused and has no direction. They may fill out the appropriate checklists and present the required PowerPoint briefings, but, when you suggest a process to follow, they typically respond, "We need to get started; we don't have time for that."

These managers are like the Hanna-Barbera cartoon character Ricochet Rabbit, who would bounce off several walls at high velocity, gleefully screaming, "Bing-bing-bing." Like Ricochet Rabbit, somehow they think that breaking their resting inertia with high velocity is going to be enough, with no thought to where they are headed.

As I frequently say to teams that are eager to just get started with little planning: If you wanted to get to New York City from Austin, you wouldn't just jump in your car and head in a generally northeasterly direction, would you? Wouldn't you:

► Check the air, the tires, and the gasoline level (resources)?
► Create a target for when you wanted to get there (schedule)?
► Try to anticipate and mitigate the risks (weather, bad roads, needed car maintenance)?
► Estimate the costs and make sure you could afford it?

Many people nod their agreement with that analogy but then are still tempted to drive their multimillion-dollar project in a generally northeasterly direction.

Actions You Can Take

If your organization underplans, you need to focus its energy with the following actions:

► Show stakeholders what the return on investment (ROI) will be. Ultimately, however you undertake planning, it must be perceived as being worth the effort involved.

► Get the commitment from your management and your team that an adequate planning effort will be undertaken. Be flexible, but stand for what you believe is right. You'd be amazed how often someone who passionately explains why a course of action is correct can persuade others who themselves have never thought deeply about the subject.

Project Pitfall: Overplanning the McClellan Way: DO-Loop to Infinity

Overplanning is the other extreme. The DO-Loop is a well-known software construct in which a software operation is performed a set number of times. A counting routine ensures that the program proceeds to other software lines after the desired work has occurred. Infinite DO-loops are programming errors that cause the program to never progress and eventually to crash.

General George McClellan, the head of the Union army during the first fifteen months of the U.S. Civil War, employed what I describe as an infinite DO-loop planning process. Refusing to strike a Confederate army (which according to independent sources had fewer than 60,000 men) that he estimated first in August 1861 at 100,000 men, at 170,000 by mid-September, and later at 200,000 troops, he continued to ask for more resources and created several battle plans, all known for their grandiosity. McClellan's delay allowed the South to prepare. Many experts think decisive action early could have led to a quick Union victory. President Abraham Lincoln, after much anguish, eventually replaced McClellan with General Ulysses S. Grant, an entirely different kind of leader. McClellan's lack of action, perhaps a result of McClellan's personal ambitions, which included a run for the presidency in 1864, frustrated Lincoln immensely, as can be seen in this ironic comment: "If General McClellan did not want to use the army, he would like to borrow it. . . ." (*Lincoln and McClellan: The Troubled Partnership between a President and his General*, by John C. Waugh [Palgrave Macmillan, 2010]).

The pitfall here is that planning for planning's sake alone, with detailed project plans that drive monstrous thousand-line-plus schedules, painfully complex risk logs, and other actions that don't enable your success, often leads to plans that are impossible to execute successfully, like those of General McClellan. A reasonably detailed plan that is achievable is absolutely necessary, but you want the size and effort of the plan to only be what is needed to enable the successful attainment of the business goals you signed up for.

Actions You Can Take

To combat any tendency toward overplanning, try these steps:

▶   To keep focused, ask this question often: "The problem we are trying to solve on this project is: _____?" Demand that the answer be only one sentence.

▶   Your organization almost certainly has a project planning process, but one size does not fit all. Follow the process, but in a way that matches your team's needs. Do not just fill out the planning tools as if they were paperwork at the doctor's office (as quickly as possible, in other words). Instead, use them to drive your agenda.

▶   Craft your own simple tools to capture the needed information, and use it to drive the correct actions, always matched to your team's maturity and needs.

▶   Think of McClellan using troop estimates that were incorrect in a way that caused constant replanning as motivation to "plan, then do' what is reasonable.

How to define what is reasonable? Ask people you respect, and actively listen to their answers. Increase your emotional intelligence through some of the means identified in Chapter 7. Take the time to sit and think things through; you don't have to simply react to the latest fire drill.

Project Pitfall: Agenda Hijack

The previous two pitfalls demonstrate extremes in planning philosophy at an organizational level. At the project level, other agendas often intrude into the project planning process. For example, Mike, a project manager for a large multimillion-dollar organization in the western United States, shared with me an example of poor planning based on a business objective that had nothing to do with the success of the project. A $20 million project concluded 2 percent over budget, a victory in itself to most people in development circles. And the project's success enabled Mike's larger organization to get substantial additional funding for the next year.

However, during planning, Mike had warned of the risk of an internal financial system that did a poor job of gathering and projecting project costs. Because of that risk, he had advised the line manager to plan only a $19 million project (rather than a potentially available $20 million budget). The line manager had not wanted to leave $1 million on the table, so he ignored Mike's advice and planned the project for the $20 million budget, ensuring another $1 million in bookings for his area. When costs were finally totaled, the project was 2 percent over the $20 million budget, requiring that more funding be procured. Had he managed to a planned $19 million project, Mike believes, the project would have overrun the target slightly also but also come in well below the max funding of $20 million. This highlights an important issue to keep in mind during planning: projects almost always spend a little more than what is budgeted.

Mike now believes he should have forced the issue of financial accountability during planning. Had he done so, the team would have appeared later to have the project well under control.

Actions You Can Take

You can take these steps to keep your project from being hijacked:

▶   Bring up key issues, like Mike's financial accountability concern, early in the process. I can't tell you the number of times people have told me, after encountering problems like this: "I knew that was going to be a problem. I just didn't say anything!" Speak up, and use your integrity to convince the audience that something needs to be done. Do not come off like a jerk; instead, if the audience won't listen this month, bring it up again using different words next month.

▶   Socialize your message through one-on-ones and hallway conversations with key decision makers.

▶   If all else fails, after a situation like Mike's, point out to all involved the lesson learned, and "do different" for next time. Help the organization learn.

Historical Planning Approaches

Enough about pitfalls for the moment. Historically, how have organizations approached the detailed planning of projects?

First, in standard hierarchical organizations—often overly structured in a functional (design vs. test, for example) way—a linear checklist or a cookbook approach to project management is often used because planners lack an understanding of the interrelatedness of the project functions. Subsequent micromanagement can drive the project manager and the team to distraction as they try to answer multiple what-if questions from stakeholders in what are often futile efforts to demonstrate that they have planned for every possible contingency. Also, functional groups are often not effectively interconnected to solve the project's problems. This silo effect, where each group works to do its task well to the detriment of the team goal, is prevalent in technical teams. Dr. Ajay C., a CAD manager from Austin, says that effective project managers have the rare ability to integrate (remember that aspect of integrity from Chapter 2?) the various silos on a team into a high-performing unit. The tendency to silo PM people into doing only schedule updates or metric status is particularly to be watched for and avoided. Because of the confusion and complexity that such silos create, once the project starts the project management implementation will likely be abandoned at the first sign of trouble, weakening the perceived value of project management in the organization.

Second, recognizing the weakness of the standard hierarchical approach, many organizations began to plan using a systems viewpoint. Systems theory as it is applied to business systems is not a new concept. Dr. Kenneth Boulding (oddly enough, the father of one of my Duke University business school professors) published the seminal paper "General Systems Theory: The Skeleton of Science" way back in 1956. *The Theory and Management of Systems* (McGraw-Hill, 1967), by Richard Johnson, Fremont Kast, and James Rosenzweig, translated general systems theory into general business theory in the 1960s.

Systems theory was quickly applied to project management. One has only to look at the subtitle of the leading project management book, Dr. Harold Kerzner's *Project Management: A Systems Approach to Planning, Scheduling, and Controlling* (Wiley, 2009), to see this. Kerzner devotes all of Chapter 2 to systems theory and concepts. He states that "the creation of a management technique that is able to cut across many organizational disciplines—finance, manufacturing, engineering, marketing, and so on—while still carrying out the functions of management . . . has come to be called systems management, project management, or matrix management (the terms are used interchangeably)." This classical system view is better than the results from standard hierarchical (functional) project structures, but something still isn't right. Modern projects just don't operate well when planned like this!

TACTILE Planning Approach

In both standard hierarchical and classical systems, information is still too isolated and doesn't flow at the near-instantaneous rate that is needed on modern projects. A successful project is best characterized not as a collection of individuals bent on perfecting their little piece of the puzzle and connected by other manager(s) but as a *learning, adaptable, dynamic organism* in which:

- ➤ Information is connected (shared) rather than hoarded.
- ➤ Thinking is big-picture, focused on a meaningful business goal internalized by the team, rather than siloed and localized.
- ➤ Cooperation within the entire team is the standard action, rather than existing only within one's clique or subteam.
- ➤ Flexibility, competency, and knowledge sharing are the group norms, rather than power and hierarchy concerns.

Project Management Plan Basics: Scope, Time, Cost, and Risk Management

How can you as the project manager plan your project so that your project is characterized by the desirable characteristics we just outlined? Let's first cover the basic ingredients for any project plan:

▶ A requirements document (scope management) with a robust change control mechanism

▶ A schedule (time management) with resource cost estimates (cost management)

▶ A risk management register used to raise and capture those risks that might impact project success

How do you keep this simple? Why, you create your plan all at once! Well, maybe not exactly all at once, but how about working on the different elements in an integrated way? First, let's look at the suggested process for building your schedule.

The Schedule Build Process

There are myriad ways to get your schedule built. Unfortunately, the approaches often seem to range from massive multimeeting and multiday events that take a great deal of time for you and the key team leaders to approaches that can be quite hands-off. Often, in these latter cases, you or your project management team perform the work alone, with input grudgingly given by managers who consider themselves too busy or too technical to get involved in planning the schedule. The former approach takes too much time and yields sometimes useful but always unwieldy implementations; the latter approach rarely does more than plant a bull's-eye on your back. I like something different: an inclusive approach that has the added benefit of not taking a great deal of time.

The tool used can be something relatively simple, like Microsoft Project. Or it may be a hugely complex tool, of which there are many. I like a simpler (not *simple*) approach.

The level of detail in a schedule may be excruciatingly high, as when you try to capture a priori everything that may be needed during the effort. Or the schedule may be built at a much higher level. Traditional thinking says, "More is better." I disagree. In my experience with development teams, the converse actually yields better results, because, with "more is better," the analytical, precise aspects of technical people's natures take over and they try to capture *everything*, which of course is not possible. This often leads to wasted effort.

I recommend what I call a milestone approach, in which you and the key managers on the team get together early and craft a schedule that plans the key milestones with enough detail that you know what is going on and also can't be accused of padding the schedule. When is enough actually, in fact, enough? When you can justify to yourselves what is on paper. When you can convince yourself you aren't *drinking your own bathwater*. And when you can present the milestone schedule to management stakeholders and withstand their probing questions. This process will require some coordination with management and other stakeholders beforehand. In fact, you'd better make sure the biggest boss around, like the division general manager, is on board.

After you have a milestone schedule that passes muster, you task the key managers with the detail planning of their subteam's tasks. You have them do this in a connected way so that they communicate with one another. You detail plan the first quarter or so of the project, and add more detail as you go forward. Note: This is more than just rolling-wave planning, the proof of which I'll leave for another time.

Now let's take a look at a tool that will help you work with your key managers to plan their tasks.

Tool You Can Use: Project Planning Template

As stated earlier, I assume your organization has committed to a particular planning tool or process. My intent is not to go down the bunny hole of comparing and contrasting them but rather to supplement whichever tool you do use.

Figure 8-2 presents a variation of what I first used on the project referred to as The Gang That Could (Finally), mentioned in Chapters 5 and 6, as a way to hold the managers on the team accountable and to get them to communicate with one another on key issues. On previous projects, the team had generated detailed schedules at the beginning of the project that really were of no help downstream; the managers wanted a simple and useful process. My approach was tailored to deal with this concern.

Before we go through each entry, here are some constraints that I push for on the schedule of any development project:

Figure 8-2: Project Planning Template

Project Name: _____   **Functional Area:** _____

Functional Manager: _____   **Today's Date:** _____

Task name	Scope document reference	Who will do it?	When will it be done?	List design tools required (Are they new?)	Other groups affected	Key risks

- Each task must take no more than eighty hours.
- Each task should be planned as if a midlevel individual contributor were going to do the work. For example, if your organization has three grade ranges for people who work at those types of tasks, assume the competency and knowledge of a midlevel person in terms of how long the task will take. This will produce a schedule that is not too aggressive and not too conservative.
- Each task must be assigned to only a single person.
- Each person can be scheduled for only one task at any one time.

The third and fourth constraints are meant to minimize the many evils of multitasking. Mike S., a project manager in New Mexico, was instrumental in convincing me of these evils. Needless to say, these constraints cause a fair amount of consternation when they are first introduced. This is because task leaders, in an effort to minimize the amount of work put into what they sometimes consider non-value-added project management work, are often tempted to create large and long tasks, resulting in a lumpy schedule. Of course, this lumpiness creates all sorts of problems downstream, most of them involving your not being able to understand what is really happening on your project, how bad it is, what to do about it, and when it might get better.

Let's quickly go through each entry. First, at the top is basic information: project name, functional area, the manager's name, and date. Simple enough.

Then come columns with these headings:

- **Task Name:** Also simple enough, as long as the constraints listed earlier are followed.

- **Scope Document Reference:** You might be surprised by the number of times project managers discover, late in the project, that "requirement 2.2.3.1.4 was not designed in." This entry allows for cross-referencing with the requirement document.

- **Who Will Do It:** One person, period. "But two people have to work on this!" you will hear. "Then it's two tasks," you reply.

What competency level do your managers assume the worker will bring to the task? As stated earlier in this chapter, I always suggest that every task be planned as if an average qualified worker were going to do the work. This deals with the inevitable optimism with which all technical people seem to plan.

▶ **When Will It Be Done:** In eighty hours or less, period. "But the task takes more than eighty hours!" you will hear. "Then it's two tasks," you reply. Get the idea? Combined with the preceding entry, this entry gives you a way to capture the task cost, which in aggregate can be rolled up to your headcount cost and total headcount.

▶ **List Design Tools Required (Are They New?):** This entry is worded in a way peculiar to the microprocessor design industry, which relies heavily on what are called design automation and other types of design tools. The operational readiness and general utility of these design tools is a major bottleneck on microprocessor projects. A generic phrasing for this entry might be *Any Use of the Item That Traditionally Bottlenecks Us?* This entry gives you risk management information.

▶ **Other Groups Affected:** This gets at dependencies and assumptions. It also allows you to drive communication, as well as risk management information.

▶ **Key Risks:** "None!" you may hear. "There must be at least one thing that keeps you awake at night," you reply. When they don't say anything but look like the proverbial deer in the headlight, you say: "Those are the risks. Just write them down."

An Earned Value Primer

When you think of the acronym EV these days, you may think first of electric vehicle. But I am actually writing about something called earned value.

This EV is an objective method used to measure the progress of a project against its plan. EV is an integral part of the professional certification offered by the Program Management Institute and is generally required on technology development projects funded by the U.S. Department of Defense (DOD).

Nevertheless, I have found resistance in commercial entities to the use of EV; the thinking is that EV is expensive and too cumbersome to implement. This need not be the case. I recommend you consider EV in planning and use it where the basic conditions outlined here apply. If you use some common sense in applying EV, you can implement it simply and effectively.

First, you need to know the basics and a few definitions. After that, I will describe a straightforward way to implement EV on your project.

Here are the basic conditions around EV:

▶ To measure progress, you must have a stable baseline. In human terms, that means a project planned the way it will be run (realizing that nothing is ever perfect) and one that doesn't change constantly. Poorly planned (or overly planned) projects will be a nightmare if you try to use EV.

▶ You need a realistic schedule. Otherwise, you will start out behind, and this will bring on an immense reporting time sink. No 10/90 schedules (10 percent nominal chance of making it).

▶ Conservative resource loading. This means minimal to no multitasking.

Next are a few short definitions. Bear with me; the internal language of EV is a bit arcane. This is where people usually lose patience with EV. I will explain clearly what each term really means.

▶ **Budgeted Cost of Work Scheduled (BCWS):** This is the plan. Each task has a BCWS equal to the task's person-hour estimate.

▶ **Budgeted Cost of Work Performed (BCWP):** This is the measure of how much work has been performed. You must have a plan for measuring progress for each task. I strongly recommend a 0/100 approach, in which no task gets any credit until completed. People who like to quickly get to 85 percent work accomplished and then seemingly can't get any further hate this guideline. However, combining this with the idea that no task should be planned for longer than two weeks, as mentioned earlier in this chapter, will keep you out of a lot of trouble.

▶ **Actual Cost of Work Performed (ACWP):** This refers to the actual cost of the work performed. All scheduling tools I have ever seen can easily calculate this (and all the other measures mentioned in this section).

Now, if you ignore the weird-sounding titles, the actual definitions don't sound so bad, do they? You had to create a plan anyway, so your BCWS had to be done. And you have to measure what you have actually done (BCWP), as well as what it cost (ACWP). And, besides, the software will be doing all the calculations. It is important that you understand the mechanics, however, and they are not complicated.

For example, at six months of a twelve-month project (50 percent), the plan (BCWS) calls for 500 staff-months worth of work to be completed. Let's say that 375 staff-months worth of work have been accomplished, or performed (BCWP), at a cost of 550 staff-months (ACWP). From these three measures, we can derive the few metrics we need.

First, compare the work performed (BCWP) against what that work cost (ACWP), by dividing BCWP/ACWP. The result is called the *cost performance index (CPI)*. In this example, CPI is (BCWP/ACWP) = (375 staff-months/550 staff-months) = 0.68. The result is less than one, and this is bad, because it means we are overspending. You can see this because the work performed cost more (ACWP) than its measured value (BCWP).

Second, divide the work performed (BCWP) by the plan (BCWS). This is the *schedule performance index (SPI)*. In this example, the schedule performance index would be (BCWP/BCWS) = 375/500 = 0.75. Notice, again the result is less than one. This means we are slipping schedule.

With both CPI and SPI less than one, you are overspending and behind schedule. If that is the case, you have real problems and need to face up to them—now. Of course, you can be in trouble in other ways, too! There are three other permutations: (1) behind schedule, under cost; (2) ahead of schedule, over cost; (3) ahead of schedule, under cost. Only this last permutation will give you no worries; the other two should be examined closely in the same way, as follows.

This early information is vital so that you can respond to what is happening, as opposed to finding out later and then having to drop into a reactive management mode. You should assign action items. For example, analyze the top five contributors to your lateness or overspending. What set of relatively near-term actions can be taken to close these tasks, allowing your team to take credit for them? Also, get your team into the habit of looking at the critical tasks to come over the next few weeks. Discuss as a team which of them may cause problems, and create mitigation plans.

There are myriad other metrics that can be generated from the basic three numbers of BCWP, BCWS, and ACWP. A partial list of other EV terms includes *Schedule Variance (SV), Cost Variance (CV), Latest Revised Estimate (LRE), Estimate at Complete (EAC), Budget at Complete (BAC), Variance at Complete (VAC), CPI/SPI, LRE/EAC, and the To Complete Performance Index (TCPI).* You should understand and make use of these applications as needed for your projects.

Frankly, a lot of confusion around EV comes from this large number of terms. They all have their place; in formal DOD systems, they are often all required, but otherwise well-intentioned and overly analytical people who often lack interpersonal skills can do enormous damage and create a lot of extra work if they are allowed to be unrestrained in how they use them.

Let's look at roles and responsibilities. We are not asking your key task leaders to do more than to plan their piece of the schedule. This represents no new work for them. If you created the right approach early enough, the tasks were planned so that you could derive useful EV results later.

One of your project controls people (or you) can run the numbers and create the analysis weekly (results should be presented weekly in execution phase). You must take ownership of the EV process and report on the results yourself in the weekly team meeting. And you must drive the needed actions, through good team discussion followed by assigned action items. I also find it useful to spreadsheet the weekly project total EV numbers and then graphically present progress. I graphically project the estimate at complete, planned budget at complete, projected work completion, and any projected schedule slippage. This has the advantage of not requiring the team to analyze all the numerical detail, while still enabling it to use the information to drive action.

You don't really need anything beyond what is written here and a scheduling tool (Microsoft Project is fine) to implement EV. For example, I used a process much like this to introduce EV to The Gang That Could (Finally), presented in Chapters 5 and 6. Sure, to boost your knowledge, confidence, and credibility with others, you can take one of the many EV classes out there. Or, easier and cheaper yet, buy a book on the subject. PMI, for example, sells several fine books that explain the basics in much greater detail.

Project Pitfall: 85 Percent Done to the End of Time

If I have seen it once, I must have seen it a hundred times. In reporting progress, task leaders report rapid progress on a task until they get to about 85 percent completion. That last 15 percent is a killer: hard to accomplish and hard on your project's progress. This is such a truism that people enthusiastically agree almost every time I mention it.

What happens on projects where this is allowed to occur? It is very simple, and also very painful. Quick progress seems to be made initially, allowing everyone a false sense of security. Then, all those 85-percent-done tasks drag on and on, with no end in sight. Management may react with Take the Hill Management or other punitive, reactive approaches. The team may all wind up working 24/7 to try to improve a situation that could have easily been avoided with the right planning approach.

Why does this occur so often? I think there are two reasons. Mostly, it's a result of the initial optimism of technical types, as they can see in their mind's eyes simple tasks that later somehow become more complicated. It also may have something to do with a tendency to underplan projects or perhaps with the difficulty of planning development work.

To deal with this, I try very hard to allow only 0/100 reporting on tasks. That means that no credit is taken (BCWP) until the task is totally completed. "Not fair," you cry. "I started accumulating cost (ACWP) when my person started working on the task. I want some credit! Otherwise, I look like I am behind."

"True," I nod. "That is why each task should require two weeks or less of work. In that way, most tasks complete in the month they were started." We discussed the particulars around task planning in the section "Tool You Can Use: Project Planning Template" earlier in this chapter, but suffice it to say that this pitfall, so common, can be avoided if you work it properly with your team beforehand.

Actions You Can Take

To avoid problems with that final 15 percent, try taking these steps:

➤ Don't try to introduce EV cold to a new organization without understanding how the benefits outweigh the risks, as well as the costs involved in introducing it. You must understand whether you have the personal power to successfully introduce EV into the culture. For example, I successfully introduced EV in one commercial organization, while I didn't even try in a subsequent company. Running the numbers on the ISAT tool presented in Chapter 7 (after the fact) shows why I didn't; I had nowhere near the same personal power in the second organization.

➤ Find ways to show task leaders who want to use the 85-percent-done method why it is in their interests to go to the 0/100 method.

Team Planning Meetings

A good planning process allows the project team to use these basic ingredients in a unified (integrative) way within a big-picture (holistic) context to enable project success.

How to do that in the real world? You should spend a few weeks getting to know people and their issues, the worlds they live in. Also, almost immediately after project approval, you should set up standing periodic meetings with your key team leaders to create the project plan. These meetings also set the tone and culture for how you will plan, execute, and monitor and control the project. Done properly, they will be seen as your meetings—with your agenda—and will naturally progress into project team meetings as you take a good plan into execution, with metrics that can be used for monitoring and controlling the project.

Key characteristics of these meetings that are crucial to their success include the following:

▶ **Attendees:** These are project staff members who are responsible for significant work or cost elements. Typically, they are functional managers for whom the individual contributors work. There are also others, such as system architects or procurement managers, who need to attend. Invite anyone who is spending money, has people on the project, or is responsible for one of the knowledge groups (the QA or HR manager, for example) or project initiatives (Black Belt champion or a quality engineer).

▶ **Agenda:** Start with actions that involve the requirements (scope) document, schedule, budget, and risk register. Don't focus overtly on the other knowledge areas: human resources, communication, quality, procurement, and integration. We will get to them; they are actually the secret sauce that will later enable your project plan to come to life. Also, these cannot be just informational meetings; you must assign appropriate action items and be sure the actions are being met. These folks are busy. They will stop coming and/or complain about the meetings if work doesn't get done—that is, if they don't get a return for their time invested.

▶ **Timing:** The meetings should take place every week. If the energy level drops, then the meeting isn't active enough. The answer is not to have the meetings less frequently. Instead, you personally need to talk less and devote more of the meeting to letting the team members work issues with one another. As you move closer to the planning completion milestone, these meetings may become more frequent, probably daily.

▶ **Duration:** You want to work the meeting duration down to one hour per week. For those of you who have planned a project, one hour may sound impossible. There may be many additional meetings going on away from your meeting, but this meeting needs to be focused. Publish the agenda each week, soon after the previous meeting—the day of the meeting, if possible. State the items to be discussed and the duration of each discussion. Then be sure to stick to the times shown on the agenda. If an item needs more discussion, put it in the bullpen and move on. If emergent issues seem to be about to hijack your well-planned agenda, try to put those issues in the bullpen to discuss after the items on your agenda. Be flexible, however, because sometimes the issue needs to be discussed at that moment. You must have the emotional intelligence to know when this is the case!

▶ **Content:** This varies over time, becoming more refined as you go forward, but the basic approach is to have all managers responsible for their own tasks estimate their own costs, raise potential risks, and close open scope issues in their areas. The managers own the subschedules they bring to the team meetings. They own their costs and risks. They close the open scope items in their areas. If they don't do this and know intimately the details in their own areas, they won't be able to work with the rest of the team. You must hold them accountable. Do not let them delegate responsibility for their schedule piece to you, your people, or members of their teams. The value-add that you provide is in getting them, over time, to better focus on the team goal and to enable the team members to work together across their silos as issues arise that cut across those boundaries. In this way, the schedule ultimately won't be just a mashed-together pastiche of each manager's subschedules; it will be a true team effort.

Finishing the Plan: Quality Assurance, Human Resources, Communication, Procurement, and Integration Management

So what about the subplans for the other five knowledge areas—quality assurance, human resources, communication, procurement, and integration management? There likely will be quite a few people on your team and within management who want to gloss over these knowledge areas. They may dismiss HR with statements like,

"That is so touchy-feely . . . we don't have time for that stuff." The quality function may be dismissed with statements like, "Those people will just slow us down with all their requirements. We know how to get a good product out the door in the real world." Procurement is often viewed as a function that can just be told what to do, a support organization that isn't truly part of the team.

The following steps will help you deal with these issues:

► Don't focus overt attention early on subplans for human resources, communication, procurement, and quality. Instead, let them develop naturally over time after a rough-draft baseline for schedule, cost, scope, and risk is sketched out.

► Be sure through your actions that the rest of the team knows that HR, procurement, and quality are important (more on communication and integration shortly). Also, be sure their representatives are part of team meetings, and solicit their input during the meetings where possible. Ask these reps to be working on their subplans, and schedule periodic reviews and discussions with each of them. Include their subplans as frequent agenda items in the weekly meeting. For example, John Berra of Emerson Process Group makes sure people understand the value of what he calls integral HR in his organization; indeed, his HR staff person is his right hand. He asks HR for direct and negative feedback on his performance as a leader to "avoid becoming isolated." I know you are not a chairperson like Mr. Berra, but see if your assigned HR team member or direct staff members will do the same for you.

► Assign the communication subplan creation to yourself. This book is all about that!

► Your approach to the overall project is the integration subplan. Describe that approach and you have it documented.

Discovering and Addressing Needed Information Until Approval

Now that when your baseline project management plan is done, you still have lots of work to do before you can get a final version of the darned thing approved. Doing a good job here means discovering and addressing new information that comes up from a variety of sources, including team meetings, hallway discussions, technical one-on-ones, and other meetings. View the process as one of refining what were essentially *best guesses* in the initial schedule, budget, and scope documents.

As we've discussed, each of the nine knowledge areas has a subplan within the overall project management plan. All too often, instead of looking at the project management plan as a system plan, management reviews of the project management plan involve the overscrutiny of individual subplans. Knowing this to be the case beforehand, the project management team spends an inordinate amount of time on what is often called PowerPoint Engineering, simply trying to make a slick presentation to come up with the right words to get the plan approved. Don't get caught up in this. Instead, focus on the issues your team raises.

We all know that technical people often prefer to work alone. But they are also passionate about their work, and therefore details of the task they are working on are likely to be the one thing they will talk about. Your role as project manager is to help the rest of the team reduce the ambiguity in those initial estimates of task duration, task content, and task cost by getting them to share their assumptions with the people affected by them.

Project Pitfall: Assumption Junction

Innate to the spirit of most technically oriented people is the desire to master some arcane set of technical knowledge. Success in this quest almost invariably means that the person has only minimally absorbed arcane knowledge from other areas. It's most beautiful indeed to watch a *sharing discussion* of deep knowledge in disparate areas between two experts who respect and understand each other.

But what happens when experienced and inexperienced people are thrown together on a dynamic, chaotic project and told to go full speed ahead? Allison G., a project manager for Intel Corporation in Folsom, California, says, "An assumptions chasm develops between the experienced and inexperienced people on the project." When problems later occur, the experienced people make statements like, "Obviously, you should know *that*" or "I just assumed you knew."

To standardize assumptions, Allison has created a process in which she meets one-on-one with the key personnel on her projects (or with everyone if team size allows) and asks them a series of questions until she pulls out of them the desired information, which is then broadly shared. The ultimate goal, of course, is to get team members to communicate with one another.

Allison has team members visualize, often "using a little movie script with them as characters," as she describes it. Only then does she show an assumptions worksheet for each person to fill out with his or deliverables, receivables, and, most important, any assumptions about those deliverables and receivables. And, yes, sometimes she fills it out for them the first time!

The information from these assumptions worksheets is used as a basis for discussion that creates the proper culture of communication. She continues to refine the information from those sheets with her teams over time. Inevitably, the sharing of information that comes about from this questioning process leads to a better *team understanding* of how the project will be executed.

I used the project planning template (Figure 8-2) shown earlier in this chapter for much the same purpose with The Gang That Could (Finally), discussed in Chapters 5 and 6. Understanding and documenting these assumptions, especially as they relate to dependencies across groups or other subteams within the overall project team, enables a more accurate planning process. Without such a process, as Allison puts it, "Even the best and brightest don't know what they each own, need, and are expected to deliver."

Of course, Allison's or any other worksheet is meant to be a supplement to a robust scheduling tool. Scheduling is obviously not a trivial task. I have been involved in projects with thousand-line schedules and seemingly endless dependencies. I once worked on a project (development of Motorola's $6 billion Iridium satellite system) that employed a large team of people just to update the schedule. Organizations often go to excruciating lengths to create what they think are good schedules.

Implicit in all this is that you are using some sort of organizational planning tool. There are many good ones out there. The best I've been exposed to may be Goldratt's Theory of Constraints because of the discipline built into using the tool, but even that tool can be overused.

Actions You Can Take

To standardize assumptions, you can try these steps:

➤ Get your team talking (communicating) about the pertinent details and the assumptions in a way that makes it seem a necessary part of their workload and not *additional* project management work.

➤ Make sure tools are viewed only as tools to serve you and the team, not as holy-grail solutions in themselves. Like Allison, be creative, and find ways to match the little aids you create to your team's personality and needs. Try something; if it doesn't work, modify it until you get something useful. None of the items I talk about are that complex. They were simply matched to the needs of the team in a way that was effective.

Too often, project managers take much more destructive approaches. For example, they may assume they know more than the technical experts, arguing from a limited viewpoint against experts in a certain area. The next pitfall relates such a story.

Project Pitfall: Management Mismanaging Your Planning

A number of years back, JT, a technical consultant from the East Coast, was the project leader for a team hired to oversee the development of a management information system (MIS) that would support operational equipment deficiencies related to the fielding of a particular global system. Previously, the deficiency reports— without any kind of improvement process in place—had just been sent out, or shot-gunned, into the maintenance organizations in the hope that engineering responses would be forthcoming. The return response rate was dismal. There was concern that these deficiency reports were essentially being ignored and that continuous improvement was not occurring.

A program manager was assigned from the engineering division of the responsible organization. He was ex-military, having previously seen combat in an overseas theater. He was smart and had a vision of how he wanted to approach the project. He articulated his vision forcefully, in a commanding style. Listening was perhaps not his strongest skill.

After a period of analysis and discussion (JT was a TACTILE-type leader), it quickly became apparent to JT and his associates that the proper course was to progressively plan the effort, which at its core involved a Web-based workflow. They spent their initial planning efforts architecting and building the information system infrastructure in anticipation of receiving from the project manager more detailed requirements from subject-matter experts familiar with the technical details.

Unfortunately, the necessary written requirements from the program manager were not forthcoming. His military background drove his thinking along strict organizational lines and command hierarchy. As brilliant as he was, the program manager did not know what he did not know, didn't listen to JT's team, and therefore did not see the need for more detail in order to take the MIS prototype to the next stage. He also displayed a volatile temperament at times, thus making it difficult for people to approach him.

An unfortunate incident occurred in a presentation by JT during a project review. Unbeknownst to JT, his colleagues had urged a subordinate to confront the program manager during JT's presentation. When this occurred, the program manager began angrily bellowing expletives at the subordinate as JT stood in front of the room. JT jokes that half the building cleared out as the program manager's words echoed down the hallway.

JT was torn. On the one hand, he had deep respect for the program manager's vision, his abilities, and his past service to his country. But the effort they were working on was to benefit the reliability of the fleet of equipment in the field, reducing risk of loss of life to those using and supporting the system. JT politely insisted that he be allowed to continue demonstrating the MIS framework. JT's planned half-hour presentation turned into a protract-ed—but productive—four-hour discussion in which the message finally got through that subject-matter experts were needed to supplement the team's expertise if the project was to proceed in a productive manner.

JT's team finally received access to and support for the needed subject-matter experts in the program manager's organization, but much time had been wasted in getting access to these people. With the added details provided by the subject-matter experts, the nec-essary increase in scope was now apparent for all to see, resulting in more funding. The program manager angrily castigated JT and his team as "thieves" as he was forced to dip into his management reserve.

In the end, the effort was successful, as a system was put in place that institutionalized accountability from the operations support personnel in the field globally all the way back to the engi-neers providing ongoing support in their comfortable offices in the United States. Thousands of users were enrolled globally.

Actions You Can Take

To avoid this kind of tension, you can take preemptive steps:

▶ To prevent yourself from getting into JT's position, scope out any new PMs or managers as they are assigned. Go meet them privately for a "get to know you" chat. Feel them out for their approach. Carefully explain to the PM the cost of the approach shown earlier.

▶ If you are in the PM's position of having responsibility for a new group, get the affected team together early and explain to the members what your expectations and work style are. Let them ask questions and discuss their concerns with you, perhaps in a later meeting after they have seen you work for a while. This shouldn't make you feel like your authority is being questioned. Eisenhower ran staff meetings like that, and he won a world war and became president!

This story was about a manager who did too much. The next

pitfall involves people who won't do enough—those who will not get involved.

Project Pitfall: "Head's Up! Here Comes the Ball!"

Have you ever watched a youth basketball team play under the pressure of a game situation? If they haven't played together in a competitive way against difficult opponents, many players who are otherwise fine in practice may exhibit some strange behaviors. For example, they may throw the ball without ensuring that there is a teammate in the vicinity of the pass. Also, some of them learn how to be where the ball isn't, without it being at all obvious that they are essentially running from the ball.

These behaviors are essentially ways to avoid the responsibility (accountability) of playing with their teammates, a behavior you may frequently see in knowledge worker teams. Getting the players on the court to work together, to pass the ball around quickly until someone has a close open shot, is the stated goal of every basketball coach, and it has a lot in common with the goal of every good project manager.

Actions You Can Take

These actions can help you teach your team members to play well together:

▶   Coach your key team leaders in the right leadership skills. Many of them have never been exposed to what it means to be a good leader. I use my weekly one-on-ones with my staff to help with this.

▶   Model the right behaviors. To me, they are the TACTILE characteristics of high integrity with transparency, accountability, and communication, which ultimately lead to trust and the right execution results through your strong leadership. Your list of behaviors may be different and should be what works for you.

▶   Catch people doing something right, and point it out to the team where possible.

▶   Hold members accountable when they act parochially.

Remember that old canard of praising in public and criticizing in private. It is amazing how often managers don't praise at all, while criticizing others frequently in public forums.

Flexibly Looking Ahead

Congratulations! Your project management plan has finally been approved. What a hassle that was, huh? Took a while, and now you feel too tired to go execute. Hate to tell you, but you still have a little bit more planning to do. Do this well, and execution is almost certain to go much better.

Planning for Execution

For optimum efficiency, planning must work in an integrated way with your execution approach. Using TACTILE characteristics (or your own) early with the team and then carrying them forward into each subsequent phase is a good start. I would hope that you have been doing so all along the way.

But what specifically can you do in planning to set the stage for execution? First of all, you need to be consistent across all the phases. While it is certainly true that each phase is distinct and has exit criteria, to be successful you need to view the entire project as one big war. If you prefer less grisly analogies, think of the project as one long game. In either case, you need a consistent game plan that is developed early and applied throughout. Winning generals, coaches, and project leaders don't usually succeed by just jumping in the fray in toxic reactive ways, as we discussed in Chapter 5.

As you are planning the project, the team meetings described earlier should be setting up eventual success by creating a winning culture, which is really just defining the way of describing how things get done. Those team meetings should be focused on the same items that you will cover, albeit in a different way, during execution. The items are the scope document, schedule, budget, and risk register, as well as any emergent issues from the other four knowledge areas of HR, communication, procurement, and quality. Of course, planning is the process where you "pierce the fog of confusion" on how the project will be managed, so you can't exactly work execution problems, but you can proactively work to understand and minimize problems in all the key areas mentioned earlier.

Planning for Monitor and Control

Additionally, you should also be planning for how you will monitor and control the project. The execution and monitor/control phases very much need to be managed in an integrated, virtually seamless way, as shown in Figure 8-1, if for no other reason than that the team members will rebel at what feels like extra reporting work if you don't do so. To be successful, you must generate data for the purpose of monitor and control that are useful to the people generating the data. This requires that your approach to the project be one of solving the team's problems, rather than *controlling* the project. Your mindset needs to be that your goal is to help them understand what problems of theirs can be solved or prevented as a result. They cannot look on you as a *controller* if you want to succeed. You need their cooperation, which they can withhold all too easily in myriad ways if you appear to be wasting their time on non-value-added work in an effort to control them and the project.

Planning the Replan

Inevitably, no matter what you do, a replan may be required. I do not define replanning as making up a plan knowing that you can't meet the deadline it includes, then waiting for the artful moment to say, "Replan needed!"

All joking aside, what differentiates normal adjustments from a new plan or a replan? Of course, in any case, you aren't going to hit every major milestone with the exact number of people estimated during planning and with all the planned features. You will tweak a bit, move a bit of work around, shift and add resources. That is, in one sentence, what you are *supposed to do* in order to do the job well.

A new plan (much more than a replan) is required when new

features are added or when key assumptions prove wrong. Most often, it is required because marketing has identified a shift in the market that requires a major new feature or because someone drastically (whether deliberately or not) underestimated an element of the original project.

The kind of replanning I am talking about lies between a new plan and normal tweaking. This kind of replanning is most often needed for risk mitigation—for example, if a design tool does not work as advertised or if assumptions about a vendor's or a remote site's ability to deliver a key component were wrong.

You need to plan for this by communicating to all stakeholders the conditions under which you will replan:

► Plan the replan at first so that it can be viewed stand-alone for scope, schedule, and cost. This means that you do not impose new schedule tasks on the old schedule. That will drive any review attendees crazy as they try to compare the old and the new plans.

► Have a risk register that addresses *only* the replan risks.

► Be conservative in your estimates. In this case, conservative means *not low*. That's right, do not lowball.

► Have a plan on how to roll the replan into your schedule going forward.

► Continue to have a way to show costs from the replan. People are going to ask.

Bottom line: be prepared, and life will be much easier for you.

Avoiding Toxic Management in Planning

Toxic management that was avoided in initiation can pop up anytime, certainly in planning. This is because both extreme forms of toxic management, Country Club Management and Take the Hill (At Any Cost) Management, are rooted in fear, and stakeholders can become afraid for a number of reasons that have nothing to do with how you are managing the project. Here are a few: (1) a key customer (friend) makes a statement about a desired new feature;

(2) another project or product in the overall portfolio performed poorly and now your project is the company's only hope for salvation; (3) a longtime high-level designer suggests that she thinks the project is struggling.

Also, all reactive management is toxic, unless the building is literally on fire. It is not rooted in good planning approaches and in a set of key characteristics that drive all actions. In reactive mode, management may involve itself in virtually all aspects of a project. It may:

▶ Demand an overly detailed project schedule and metric set that includes *everything*.

▶ Intensely scrutinize all aspects of the project schedule and metrics, demanding that managers track infinitely small details.

▶ Use *in-your-face* accountability in lieu of creating a mutually accountable culture.

▶ Do whatever is necessary (wheedling, browbeating, driving, quietly dropping scope) not to miss a scheduled milestone.

▶ Ask itself, you, your team, and family members to sacrifice everything for the project.

▶ Completely control all information into and out of the project, especially bad news, such that nothing potentially helpful can be done by anyone else.

Your customer may resort to some of these same approaches and apply them, unbeknownst to you, through your management channel. Your team will not respect you if it sees you being managed this way. It will also begin to act and feel less open and trusting.

This book is meant to give you approaches that will enable you to avoid using toxic management styles yourself and to avoid being managed that way.

Case Study: The Path Less Taken

The planning phase is where things begin to get interesting with our team and the two approaches by which it is managed. The standard approach (Ravi's team) begins to show some strains, while Sheila's TACTILE approach is a bit of a struggle. Over time, however, Sheila's team is beginning to reap the rewards of its open and straightforward culture.

Standard Approach

Month 1 of Planned Eighteen-Month Project
Hallway Conversation

Bennett (never Ben) Lee shakes his head tersely. "I can't do that BS, Ravi. I got people working and stuff to do. Every morning for two weeks to plan Alpha O is just crazy."

"You work for me, Bennett." Ravi pauses. "Look, you've been here a long time. This came from the division staff meeting. Mark is concerned about our past poor performance. Sebastian was there, and he agreed. We have to get back on track. Be there at eight Monday in Mountain Trout conference room. And be ready. This is our chance to shine." Ravi heads down the hall.

To his back, Bennett says sotto voce, "Your chance to shine, maybe. This is overkill even by BTC standards."

Later that day...
Sebastian's Office

"Fine, as long as you use APS [All Problems Solved], the new scheduling tool we spent a small fortune on," Sebastian says. "Are four project controls people going to be enough?"

"I do not know this," Ravi replies. "Two more might be better. APS is not simple to use."

"Six people to do nothing but the schedule and metrics? For that we need a project management office of six people? Can Leanne even manage that many people?"

"This project has to succeed, yes? And you insist we use this new APS?"

"That's right." Sebastian smiles tightly. "Go ahead. I'll sign the requisitions."

Two weeks later...
Team Planning Meeting, 8 A.M.

Ravi stands. "You have worked hard on the schedule. Today is the day we were supposed to be done, but we are still not there. We will work Saturday and Sunday, and every day after until we are done." The room is ominously quiet. No one reacts. They had anticipated this. "Leanne, the floor is yours."

Leanne Taylor, nominally called the program manager but in practice only the lead scheduler, comes forward. She connects her computer to the overhead projector. "Here's the schedule as it stands. Everyone on my team worked all night again to put your changes in. But, as you can see, we still have a bunch of opens."

Still no reaction.

Leanne looks at Lance Rollins, the lead logic designer, who avoids eye contact. Somewhat wearily but still determined, she says, "Lance, as you can see on line 621, your output still isn't connected to anything. Where do you want to put it?"

Lance finally looks up. "Leanne, do you really want me to answer that?"

The cynical laughter is almost a relief.

Later in the same meeting…
11:45 A.M.

"One more argument to resolve," Ravi thinks. He stands. "Okay, everybody. Listen to me." He looks at Rajesh Kumar, his design for test (DFT) lead. "Rajesh, I know DFT is important. But you cannot be serious in continuing to ask for all of this. The time is impossible."

Rajesh frowns. "They just don't get it," he thinks dejectedly. His book *Design for Test: Microprocessors and Wireless Mobile Devices Made Cheaper* is the leading book on the subject, well, in the world. Seemingly every day, his editor or agent e-mails the news that another engineering department has adopted his book for one EE master's course or another.

More coldly than he means to sound, Rajesh says, "Ravi, Bennett, Lance, everyone. If you do not apply design-for-test principles fully in the design phase, our cost will ultimately be much higher, it will take longer to qualify the part—"

"Rajesh, Rajesh." Bennett (never Ben) Lee lifts a hand, which he shakes quickly to stop Rajesh. "No one doubts any of that. We all drank the Kool-Aid on DFT." A couple of chuckles come from around the room. "But we simply can't afford the time and effort to do everything you are asking for."

Rajesh draws himself up tightly. "And, pray, Bennett, tell us yet again why this is? Other than it saves you time in design."

Ravi squirms in his seat at the front of the room. He shares a forlorn look with Leanne.

Three weeks later...
Month 3 of Planned Eighteen-Month Project
Chilean Sea Bass Conference Room, 10:30 P.M.

Leanne types an entry into the schedule projected on the screen in the front of the room. She looks up, a weary smile on her face. "We're done, gang." They begin to stand and move toward the doors. "One thousand and thirty-three lines, but I think it's all in here. And our sixth person for the PMO will be here next week. We'll be busy, but you've got a schedule! Good job."

No one smiles, not even Ravi when she turns to him.

He just looks at her. "Three weeks late," he thinks, "and this monster of a schedule will be out of date in two weeks. How did this happen?"

Leanne wearily walks over to him. "Now we get to go fight with the staff over approval to leave planning, huh, Ravi?" All she gets in return is a tired, rueful smile.

TACTILE Approach

Month 1 of Planned Eighteen-Month Project
GM Mark Simpson's Office

Mark looks appraisingly at Sheila. "So, how have your first few weeks been?"

Sheila laughs ruefully. "It's been interesting, Mark. *Really* interesting."

"Lance quit yet? Bennett firebombed your car?" They share a smile.

Sheila looks down briefly, then back up at Mark. "I am still on track. I've talked to some of the staff already; will get to the rest of them this week. I thought Sanders Turner was screwed up, but this isn't really even a team. They all try to do their own thing to the max and then point the finger at somebody else."

"Just as we discussed." Mark smiles tightly at her.

"Right. I did talk to Ravi last week. He seems fine for the guy who didn't get the job."

"Ravi will be fine. He's a good man. Just not the right one for what we are trying to do. He's taking his sabbatical; it's only a couple of years late. Then he wants to transfer, maybe to Systems. We'll see."

Sheila nods her head slightly in acknowledgment. "Mark, there is going to be trouble when I have the planning kickoff."

"Not a surprise, I suppose. When is it?"

"Two weeks from Thursday."

"Why so long from now? And what kind of trouble?"

"I'm taking the time to finish up my chats. And the team is finishing the open TBDs. As for the trouble, I am convinced a couple of these guys might quit. I am not sure they *can* change. Even for engineers, some of them are inflexible."

"Just used to doing things a certain way that they think works well. Maybe it once did, but times they have a-changed. Right?"

"Most definitely."

They smile tightly at each other and turn to other topics.

Same day...
Sheila's Office Cubicle, 2:00 P.M.

"Hi, Tom. Come on in." Sheila extends her hand. Tom Thompson, her layout manager, shakes it somewhat cautiously.

"It's nice to talk with you," Tom says. "I usually see *you* people only when there is a problem."

"My pleasure, Tom. I'm meeting with as many people as I can over the next few weeks to make sure I understand what is going on."

"Not a lot to know. I'm just the layout guy."

Sheila smiles. "Can't do much without a good layout, Tom. I know *that* much."

Tom warms to her. "True, I guess."

"Absolutely true, Tom. The layout guy on my last project at Sanders Turner saved our bacon." Sheila appraises him. He looks calmly back at her. "So what are we dealing with here, Tom?"

He shifts a bit in his seat. "Honestly?"

"Yes. Please."

"Dealing with a freaking nightmare, as usual. All in a day's work, I guess."

"What would make it better? The 'nightmare,' as you say?"

"Well. Same as I told the last guy in your job. Not going to change, as far I can see." Tom looks at her, pauses, and takes the plunge. "I know you're not going to believe me when I tell you this, but—"

Sheila frowns slightly as she holds up a hand. "Wait," she says softly. "Tom, wait a second. Is there something in my demeanor or attitude that makes you think I won't believe you?"

Tom freezes. "What?"

"Tom, I trust you to tell me the truth as you see it, and, if you think you can trust me, let's go on. I'll believe you, until proven otherwise. Okay?"

Tom looks oddly at her. "Sure, Sheila. Of course I trust you. It's just the last guy . . ."

"Tom, it's pretty clear I'm not the last *guy*, right?"

He nods, and smiles slightly.

"Fine. If the last guy in this job didn't believe or trust you, well, then that was his problem. I find it a lot easier to just believe people than to distrust everyone and have to deal with what comes from that. Make sense?"

"Sure. That'll be new."

Sheila smiles. "Right. Then just tell me the issues that are going to bite you, you being the same as us. How about that?"

They settle in for a nice—*productive*—discussion.

Two weeks later...
Project Planning Kickoff, 9:00 A.M.

"Morning, everyone," Sheila says in her most businesslike manner.

As usual, they sit there not interacting, checking e-mails mostly. She begins to display the agenda.

As she starts to speak, Lance Rollins, her logic design manager, interrupts. "How long is this really going to take? You can't really do a project-planning meeting in an hour. I've got another meeting I couldn't move," he concludes flatly.

"Challenge number n," Sheila thinks. She looks at Lance. "The meeting will be done in an hour," she says. She looks around the room with a slight smile on her face. "Anyone else have any concerns?"

"Another meeting," Bennett (never Ben) says flatly.

"Yep, an important meeting to plan this project."

"In all honesty, Sheila, we've got a lot of work to do."

"And no time for meetings?"

"Right."

She looks around the room. "Others feel that way?"

In response come a couple of wary nods. The mood of the room isn't with her; it isn't against her, either. "I actually didn't ask Lance to make that statement, but it is a perfect segue. We have to plan the project somehow, right?"

Most people nod. There are a few holdouts, primarily Bennett (never Ben), Lance, and her DFT manager, Rajesh Kumar. She focuses her attention on them.

"I didn't lead you astray on the pre-planning process, did I? Didn't that go well?" She pauses.

Stronger nods come from around the room. Her three holdouts are still mostly unmoved, offering slight, tight nods.

"We are going to plan, in a simple, effective way, just like pre-planning. Let me get into the agenda for what I call 'The Plan for the Plan.' " She flips on the projector. "You should have received these slides a couple days ago.

"First, as a group we will work out the top-level milestones for the project. That will take two weeks. To do this, we will meet for two hours on Monday and then ninety minutes each day for the rest of the two weeks. No weekend meetings, but you will have plenty of other meetings among yourselves to work out whatever details come up in our meetings. That's up to you.

"Second, you will create your own subschedules, using the eighty-hour/one-person-per-task rule. You get a week for that.

Then we all get back together and see if that has affected the milestone schedule. One of the people from project controls, Scott Williams, will work with you on any issues. We will use Ultracool Project, which is a plenty good enough schedule/cost tool for any project short of the Hoover Dam. Leanne Taylor has been assigned to Summit Finder, the new-generation microprocessor that is in Tech Readiness. Everyone else in what was the project controls group has been reassigned to various other projects. We won't need them. Some of you can have that headcount as needed."

She pauses. They are all listening. Perhaps Rajesh has softened a bit. Lance and Bennett are, if anything, tighter in their body language.

"Scott will be up here shortly with more detail, but you own your schedules, costs, risks, and scope. I will hold you accountable for them. Scott will help you work together, but he won't do your work for you. Don't even try to make him responsible for your schedule or risks." She looks around the room. "Grudging respect up to outright admiration," she thinks.

"Extra work for us," Bennett says.

Sheila looks him right in the eye. "Not extra. This is *the* work for you managers. You are much more than just technical experts." Sheila pauses, then starts to count on her fingertips. "My job will be to:

- ▶ Create the right culture, way of working together, process, whatever you call it.
- ▶ Help remove the obstacles you cannot remove.
- ▶ Identify and focus on the overriding team goal in all we do.

Your individual functions are important, of course, but we don't ship DFT or Design Assurance or Logic. We ship the finished product that the customer is willing to pay for. Any questions?"

Sheila answers all their questions patiently and honestly. This takes a while, but the meeting finishes on time. Lance nods his approval with a slight upward movement of his head in her direction as he leaves the meeting. Even Bennett looks less arrogant than normal. Several people look happy at work for the first time in a long time.

"Onward and upward," Sheila thinks.

Three weeks later...
Division Gate Review for Planning Approval
"This is the last slide," Sheila says. "As you can see, we are on target; we finished planning on time. We have a list of remaining action items that are manageable as we go into execution. The remaining open TBDs have been converted into risk-mitigation strategies. I request approval to leave the planning phase."

There is no dissent.

TACTILE Analysis

Sheila seems to be struggling much less than Ravi. When projects go well—when your approach is going well—you just seem to meet less resistance from day to day. Look for this on your projects, and, if you don't see it, make some adjustments until that interpersonal friction decreases.

▶ **Transparency:** Sheila's conversation with Tom Thompson, the layout manager, best shows her effort to be transparent in all her actions. Ravi's problem isn't so much a lack of transparency as it is, as with so many of the TACTILE characteristics, a failure to understand the value of having a consistent set of traits that guide his leadership efforts. His main mode of operation is just to doggedly push ahead. This may get him there eventually, but the way he gets there will not be efficient and will leave his team angry and confused.

▶ **Accountability:** Sheila holds herself and her team members accountable. Some of them, such as Bennett and Lance, don't much like it, but you can see by the end of the section that even they are beginning to understand. Ravi tries to hold his team accountable, but he doesn't understand that there is a difference between micromanaging the results and following Sheila's way of creating the right environment by being forthright about her expectations, clearly assigning responsibilities, and trusting in her team to meet those responsibilities.

▶ **Communication:** Ravi communicates near-term goals well, but he isn't very good at communicating to create personal commitment in others. His approach is that of a taskmaster who has little empathy or overall leadership ability. He lacks the emotional intelligence to bring out the best in his team. Internally, he is frustrated a large percentage of the time. Sheila, on the other hand, spends a lot of time communicating. In fact, communicating well seems to be one of her best skills. Her approach is more that of a coach with a solid game plan than that of a manager just telling her people what to do. To Sheila, communicating means actively listening and tying what she hears back into her actions.

▶ **Trust:** There is very little trust on Ravi's team. There is also an overreliance on the APS tool. But, as National Instruments VP Mark Finger says, "It doesn't matter how great your PM tool is if people don't trust each other." Conversely, the seeds of strong trust are being planted by Sheila with her team, but perhaps even more so with her management. We have seen no customer interaction so far with either Ravi or Sheila, but that will change as we proceed into project execution.

▶ **Integrity:** Ravi very much wants his team to succeed, and he is honest in a certain way (if rough) in his approach. The issue is that he doesn't try to figure out how his people think, the frustrations and challenges they face. He is not consciously working to motivate his team to peak performance; he doesn't understand the value of building and maintaining his personal integrity. Sheila, on the other hand, focuses a great deal on those things. It is not that she only talks about touchy-feely things, either. The art in what she does is that she works these people issues simultaneously with project issues.

▶ **Leadership:** Ravi is not an effective leader. He is driving his team the best way he knows how, but he lacks the tools and the emotional intelligence to get the most out of them, which leaves them feeling frustrated and rudderless. On the other hand, Sheila's team has a strong sense that they are being led somewhere that might just be good for them. Of course, they are not 100 percent in agreement about this, and there are various forms and levels of resistance. But there are also several people who are beginning to like it.

▶   **Execution Results:** Clearly Sheila has generated better results to date than Ravi, both from her team's and from her management's point of view. Will she be able to translate this into a better-performing team in execution? Some doubters would surely say, "Maybe she can plan well. Many bureaucrats can do that. But wait until she gets into execution, when the really tough technical decisions have to be made." We'll see if laying a TACTILE foundation will pay off with results.

A plan, even a well-crafted one, will get you only so far. Execution is where all your work comes together in active, ever-changing realities you will have to integrate into a seamless, functioning whole. The next chapter shows you how.

CHAPTER 9

Executing

EXECUTING IS ALL ABOUT *doing*, about meeting the schedule, performance, and cost objectives that the sponsoring organization has chosen for your project, balanced optimally with the expectations of your customer, management, and team. A clear, concise project plan, as discussed in Chapter 8, is essential, but it is only the start. Succeeding in execution means:

- ▶ Executing to the plan
- ▶ Controlling change control
- ▶ Selling new baselines
- ▶ Learning how to win

Executing to the Plan

You worked hard to get your plan approved, jumping through the myriad organizational hoops. Your plan has an impressive-looking schedule, a risk register full of the key project risks, and a budget with detailed cost estimates. You've closed a multitude of open scope items in your requirement document. You think you are ready to go.

In Chapter 1, we discussed the high failure rate of projects, mentioning that only 30 to 50 percent of projects succeed. This low number apparently has been true for a long time, as the following two quotes from the *Harvard Business Review on Managing Projects* (Harvard Business School Press, 2005) illustrate. Nadim F. Matta and Ronald N. Ashkenas, co-authors of the essay "Why Good Projects Fail Anyway," assert that "projects fail at an astonishing rate. . . . . They frequently deliver disappointing returns—by some estimates, in fact, well over half the time." As David Davis, author of the essay "Beware of False Economies," says, "New projects, especially those involving high technology, are prone to cost over-runs that may double, triple or even quadruple the original esti-mates."

This low success rate of technology development and IT proj-ects has become almost accepted. When faced with hard, cold data that my teams had completed seven microprocessor core projects in a row on time and with high customer satisfaction, one VP said, "That is impossible in this business. You must have padded the schedules or they were too easy to start with." He couldn't accept that the problem was solvable with good leadership skills and an approach based on input from the people doing the work. I won-der if the project leaders who did not achieve success started out thinking they would be successful. One can only assume so, but what happened to them?

Allison G. of Intel Corporation in California says that failure occurs when teams are unable to understand and incorporate the customer's needs and desires into their designs. Mike S. from New Mexico points out that failures are higher when "the project man-ager has limited access to the customer or when projects are understaffed due to lack of proper prioritization for the organization's key projects." Bob Carroll, consultant and author from Arizona, says, "I never had a project fail with a good project leader and a plan. I could imagine a project failing, though, which was bid too low or had upper-management constraints or interference."

Today, every organization has access to a host of expensive tools and processes, but tools and processes alone do not drive success. If they did, the success rate for projects would be much higher. Next, we'll examine two high-level pitfalls you must avoid if you don't want to become another statistical casualty in the project management jungle.

Project Pitfall: The Danger of Constant Firefighting— Executing the Grant Way

In Chapter 8, we discussed the ineffective continuous planning of General George McClellan. Essentially, McClellan never got to execution! General Ulysses S. Grant, a man with a completely different style, replaced McClellan, and their results differed as much as their methods.

Grant's approach to execution was to attack. And his approach, though costly in manpower and resources, worked. The United States did win the war under Grant's leadership, and Grant was later rewarded, becoming the eighteenth president of the United States.

The project management approach I call Take The Hill (At Any Cost) Management, which we explored in Chapter 5, is similar to Grant's approach. I am not qualified in any sense to comment on Grant's approach to war. My point is that the world of project management, jungle though it is, is not really a battleground, and our people are not warriors. Companies in the tech field, and they are numerous, that manage their people this way may succeed in some sense of the word—define success however you like—but at what cost to the employees and their families?

If the project does nominally succeed and the organization is too focused on results at any cost, this kind of forced-march approach may be widely applauded, reinforcing the behavior within the culture. Ignored are the people costs: (1) stress to the team members and their families; (2) lack of growth for other managers, since the lead manager made all the decisions; and (3) lack of a consistent team process that will work in the future without continued micromanagement.

Projects can also veer toward complete chaos, where things just blow up and fly apart. Characterized by finger pointing and stories that describe the same set of events completely differently, depending on the storyteller's viewpoint, these chaotic projects can destroy careers. *Tiger teams*, composed of senior managers and other experts who possess certain specific needed skills or knowledge, are often brought in to fix these projects. And management, believing that "discipline is needed," frequently brings in a successful forced-march manager to straighten things out after such a catastrophe.

Actions You Can Take

Avoid this pitfall by managing your teams in a people-centric manner, not just for results at any cost. To do so:

➤ Read about people-centric management systems elsewhere. Two highly recommended books are *Peopleware: Productive Projects and Teams*, by Tom DeMarco and Timothy Lister, and *Managing the Test People: A Guide to Practical Technical Management* (Rocky Nook, 2007), by Judy McKay. Grant's approach might be correct in some circumstances, but projects aren't war. Creating a calm but action-oriented culture where people can work efficiently is the best way to get things done. Resist trying to be the hero in the firefight.

Project Pitfall: Pain-Avoiding Animals

During project execution, communication is crucial—that is, critical information must move virtually instantaneously from wherever it is to wherever it is needed. One of your most important tasks is to make sure that occurs. This means that your team members do the following:

- ▶ Raise potential problems (risks) that might occur.
- ▶ Proactively share information that is needed for everyone to do a good job.
- ▶ Ask for help when they can't handle some aspect of their work by themselves.

If you don't create the right project culture so that these actions occur, your people will start to behave like pain-avoiding animals. I use this term as a way to explain seemingly irrational behavior. A few examples: "Why did he hide that the design tool was broken?" Pain-avoiding animal—he didn't want the beating that was going to come whenever the problem was found out. "Why did she not ask for help?" Pain-avoiding animal—she didn't want her manager to think she couldn't handle the task. "Why didn't he tell the right person in another group about a problem that would impact that group?" Pain-avoiding animal—he didn't want that person to yell at him (kill the messenger) for adding another problem to the other group's already large stack of problems.

The insidious part about pain-avoiding behavior is that it can be hard to detect, so it is best to stop it before it starts. People, by the time they reach the workforce, are very good at hiding how they really feel if they think they can't be open and honest.

Actions You Can Take

These actions will prevent pain-avoiding behavior:

▶ Create transparency, accountability, and communication with integrity on your team (and in all your relationships). Then trust will grow, and you will have a team that can function at a high level without a lot of intervention.

▶ Talk about pain-avoiding behavior, and try to raise awareness that you want to know the truth. You will be surprised how people will open up if you tell them sincerely that you want to know what their problems are.

▶ To minimize pain-avoiding behavior, be prepared to accept any problem raised by the team at any time. Don't kill the messenger who bravely decides it is time to tell you something late on the Friday of a holiday weekend. Thank him, and listen actively.

TACTILE Execution Approach

As I noted in the first paragraph of this chapter, execution is all about getting things done. Your whole approach to your project should be one of facilitating your team's success in getting the needed tasks completed. This is very much in the spirit of consensus decision making that is followed at National Instruments. As HR VP Mark Finger says, "We might be slower for a decision, but our execution is much better as a result." Similarly, some of what you will read in this section may seem to slow your decisions, but my experience has been in line with Mr. Finger's. Follow a similar process and you also will get superior results.

You do this through your project's key functional managers, each of whom owns a key function or area within the learning, adaptable, dynamic organism otherwise known as your team. To drive success:

► Discuss your approach with your key managers early.
► Hold an all-hands kickoff meeting.
► Continue periodic and focused team meetings.
► Use simple tools like the Yes/No Questions and Key Manager's One-Pager, both of which are discussed later in this chapter.

Key Managers Discussion

Especially if you are new to the team and the organization, you need to host a key managers' discussion before you have an all-hands kickoff meeting. This is to give your key managers a chance to express any anxiety they have about the approach and for you to incorporate what they say into the all-hands agenda. This also gives you an opportunity to try out your part of the presentation and to clarify with them what each of them will say at the all-hands meeting.

All-Hands Kickoff

A successful all-hands kickoff will introduce you and your plan to the broader organization and to your team. It will give you a leg up on transparency, accountability, and communication and allow you to begin the process of growing the trust that is so necessary in creating a high-performance team. Here are some guidelines:

▶ Everyone who works on the project should attend. This point must be driven home hard with your key managers.

▶ Senior managers who have a stake in the success of the project should attend and interact before and after the meeting with individual contributors and other team members. The most senior manager (the big kahuna) should speak briefly and demonstrate his or her personal accountability in a way that won't be cynically dismissed. This person should try very hard to attend the entire meeting and to interact with the team. Typically, if senior managers do attend these meetings, they speak at the beginning for five minutes and immediately leave. What message does that send? From among the other senior managers, only the top person in the performing organization should speak—*briefly*—perhaps to "bless" the meeting and to introduce the big kahuna.

▶ Supporting central organizations (such as subcontracting, procurement, factory, and contracts) should be invited. They may not be able to attend, but they will uniformly appreciate being invited. If they cannot attend, you should attempt to share the presentation with them later.

▶ The meeting itself should move quickly, lasting no more than sixty to ninety minutes. Key project team managers should each speak for five minutes about their functional area and plans, if possible. You should be the emcee for the occasion. You speak first, you introduce each major area, and you close the meeting. You should cover in detail the process that the team will follow to be successful.

▶ Contents of the meeting should consist of introductory

speeches; an overview of the project—that is, why it is important to the business and what the planned outcome is for the project; the process by which the project will be managed; a brief technical approach; the schedule, cost (budget), open scope issues, and risk register and other parts of the project management plan; and the applicable standards (the leading one is usually quality). Leave plenty of time for questions.

Kicking off the project like this gives you a chance to accomplish several things:

► Demonstrate your transparent approach to leadership. To drive accountability, I tell my teams what they can expect of me and the management team, as well as what is expected of them. The entire meeting shows the value of communication. Doing all this continues to build trust with your entire team.

► Educate the team members on something they are going to spend the next several months of their lives sweating over.

► Focus the energy of the team.

► Dispel any rumors or misconceptions that are driving negative energy on the team. The best way to do this is by patiently answering any and all questions they have.

Meetings

Often, people greet the approach just described with a woeful-sounding statement: "More meetings?" Next we will examine two pitfalls that commonly occur regarding meetings. Knowing about the first pitfall will help you deal with any complaining that may come your way from new meetings. The second pitfall involves a key tendency of technical teams that, if left unchecked, will waste time and dissipate energy from your team. After the two pitfalls, we will discuss how you should conduct a team meeting and take a look at the Yes/No Questions and Key Manager's One-Pager worksheets.

Project Pitfall: Meetings, Meetings, and More #!@& Meetings...

A constant refrain you will hear as you try to add discipline to the chaos of your project environment is a complaint about too many meetings. Organizations do indeed have too many meetings, meetings that often have no clear purpose, detailed agenda, or set time span and that may even lack a clear invite list. People may have been meeting to ostensibly solve problems; but all too often meetings are held out of inertia or to show that something is being done. Worst of all, the meetings don't provide lasting solutions for the problems that are driving attendees crazy. As a result, when you come in and want to start other meetings, they may balk, possibly even refusing to attend.

Actions You Can Take

Take these actions to ensure that your meetings are effective rather than out of control:

▶ Publicize any meeting well before the date of the meeting via e-mail announcement, one-to-one invitations, and appropriate mention in public forums such as operations reviews.

▶ Clearly state the purpose and what will be accomplished in every meeting.

▶ Hold the meetings as announced, with the announced duration.

▶ Publish updated action lists as soon as possible after the meeting concludes, that day if at all possible.

▶ Stick to the agenda. Bullpen any emergent issues that threaten to destroy your agenda.

▶ Ensure that your meetings are aligned with the day-to-day problems your team faces.

▶ Create a culture in your meetings where you talk relatively little—providing overall guidance and tone, making decisions only after discussion—to encourage your team to share information and problem-solve together.

➤   Limit attendance to those you think should attend. Many people attend meetings to be in the know or to protect their or their organization's backside. Then, oddly enough, they may complain about having to attend too many meetings. If attendees aren't there to actively solve problems, in most cases you don't need them. Of course, if one of your key managers brings a subordinate to explain some issue, that is fine. Get in the habit of asking about any other additional attendees. Be ready to un-invite non-value-added attendees. Be careful, of course, to do this only as absolutely required, and be sensitive to the perception that your actions are punitive in nature.

These actions will signal to people in your organization that things are going to be different, in a way that will likely yield better results.

Project Pitfall: The Seemingly Endless and Infinitely Detailed Techie-Talk Team Meeting

This pitfall deals with a type of team meeting that you need to avoid—one in which your managers describe their (and their team's) work at too great length.

Don't get me wrong; I like technical people. As a degreed engineer and member of the Electrical Engineering honor society who practiced engineering for at least a few years before going over to the "dark side" of management, I think I understand and even empathize with them. I don't consider the term *nerd*, for example, to be particularly derogatory. I know some fantastic nerds; there are probably a few in my extended family. I might even be one.

Technical people get things done that provide value to our civilization, every day, without much fuss. But they do have a couple of distinguishing characteristics that may drive you crazy: they go into too much detail, and their goals are to do everything perfectly today without too much concern about what that does to the long-term outcome (schedule and cost) of the project. Even technical managers, who should realize their job is to manage and lead, are susceptible to this.

This means that, when the technical people who are your key managers are left to their own devices in a team meeting, they may happily have the *Seemingly Endless and Infinitely Detailed Techie Talk Team Meeting*. Translated, they will have a great time giving each person the opportunity to go on and on, in seemingly infinite detail, about everything his or her team did that week. Much precious time is wasted, and they typically are not solving problems. Any input from others is often just academic advice, such as "Did you try this?" And, worst of all, anyone not interested in the topic of the moment is likely to tune out, checking e-mail or idling. In any case, during these technical deep dives, they are not working as a team.

Why does this occur? Dr. Ajay C. says, "The attitude is that I will care about my schedule when that is what I am held accountable for. If my project manager is schedule driven, I will be. If he or she is technically focused, then I will be. They set the tone. Technical debates that occur with no context happen so frequently because they are what those project managers value."

Actions You Can Take

These actions will help you keep your technical wizards' feet on the ground and their heads in the game:

▶   You are chief nerd herder. Be sure to explain what you value and verify that it matches what is truly in the organization's best interest—that it meets stated business goals.

▶   Technical people drone on about technical detail because it is what they understand best. Help your team deal with ambiguity better; nerds tend to perfectionism. Coach them that excellence is the goal, not perfection.

The next section models the kind of team meeting I have found to be effective.

Weekly Team Meetings

Team meetings in execution are a natural extension of the team meetings that were so instrumental in creating your project management plan during the previous phase. Your approach should be similar but also different in important ways:

▶ **Attendees:** This should be the same as for the planning-phase team meetings: the project key functional managers responsible for the significant work or cost elements that represent the work performed by the individual contributors. Again, as in planning, invite anyone who is spending money, has people on the project, or is responsible for one of the knowledge groups (QA or HR manager, for example) or project initiatives (Black Belt champion, for example).

▶ **Agenda:** You personally should show the near-term schedule and provide an update on any key metrics. A key project controls person may do some of this on your behalf, but you must set the tone and comment on where the project is overall. This shows your accountability and overall connection. Then there should be a discussion of each manager's Key Manager's One-Pager worksheet (see Figure 9-2 later in this chapter) for actions needed around the requirements (scope) document, schedule, budget, and risk register in relation to the near-term milestones. This should be followed by a discussion on the major risks to longer-term milestones. It remains essential that each manager be accountable for driving needed actions and that they own their subschedules, costs, scope, and risks. They must be at each team meeting to report and discuss. They cannot be allowed to delegate responsibility. How they get the work done, of course, within their own teams is their business. Finally, like in planning, these cannot be just informational or technical deep-dive meetings; you must assign appropriate action items and be sure the actions are being met. These folks must get a return for their time invested.

▶ **Timing:** Every week. Periodic key events, like meetings, enable the rhythm needed for success.

▶ **Duration:** One hour per week. Schedule the first few for ninety minutes, and then work them down to the sixty-minute goal. As repeatedly mentioned, these meetings need to be action oriented and focused—no wandering dialogues or diatribes.

► **Your Role:** As in planning, the value-add that you provide is in getting your key managers, over time, to better focus on the team goal and to enable the team to work together across their silos as issues arise that cut across those boundaries. As the various key managers cover their one-pagers, you should ask questions geared to drive a *team-oriented thought process* and to integrate ideas into solutions. Keep in mind four goals when asking these questions:

1. Encourage them to talk together so that they work better together.
2. Use the questions to uncover new risks or to gain a better team understanding of existing risks.
3. Ensure that the team is focusing clearly on near-term schedule milestones.
4. Ensure that the team is thinking about potential emergent risks.

Tools You Can Use: Yes/No Questions Worksheet and Key Manager's One-Pager

To support efficient team meetings, I recommend two simple tools, the *Yes/No Questions* worksheet (see Figure 9-1) and the *Key Manager's One-Pager* (see Figure 9-2), as the most efficient, least onerous ways to get out on the table the data that the team (and you) needs to get the job done. At the root of these tools are communication and accountability. Trust will follow when the team members start working together on the data that come from using these tools.

On every project there is a set of key managers, each of whom is responsible for some piece of your project. Those key managers should themselves fill out these worksheets. They use the Yes/No Questions Worksheet to help prepare the One-Pagers, which they will share at your team meeting each week.

Let's first look at the Yes/No Questions Worksheet. This set of questions is grouped around requirements, tools, schedule, and risks. Obviously, you can modify the list of questions for your projects. For example, if you are managing to a firm-fixed budget, you might include cost as one of the questions.

The intent of this worksheet is to remove ambiguity when the task leader or functional manager tries to fill out the Key Manager's One-Pager. If the answer to any question in Figure 9-1 is No, then the manager is driven to enter the needed action into the One-Pager. For example, if the answer to the question "Do current requirements = baseline?" is No, that means there must be a new requirement, not previously scoped, planned, costed, or risk analyzed. That means an action is required of someone. Not catching these kinds of situations early leads to a lot of rework on projects. I coach my teams that if the answer to *any* of these questions is no, then they must list what the recovery plan is for the issue raised. Note that they themselves are not always the owner of subsequent action items, but they are accountable for identifying the responsible person and demanding action until resolution.

Figure 9-1: Yes/No Questions Worksheet

Requirement: Do current requirements = baseline?

Tool: Are the tools performing as needed?

Schedule: (top-level first, then detail)

➤ Did you accomplish last week's tasks?

➤ Are you going to accomplish this week's tasks?

➤ Can you make next week's tasks on time?

➤ Delivery / milestone date ok?

Risk:

➤ Risk list complete?

➤ Is the risk list being acted on?

If the answer to any of these questions is No, what is your recovery plan?

If you don't have control of the problem, identify who does and demand resolution.

The Key Manager's One-Pager is the primary way I get team members to quickly and succinctly communicate their key issues. I ask each key manager on the project staff to fill out and present one of these at each weekly team meeting. Once this type of information is put on the table, internal commitment to the overall team goal is much easier to achieve. The information presented generates team discussion about what the team may need to do as a result. The information is presented in an action-oriented, can-do way, not as a technical status report.

The entries are fairly straightforward, but let's discuss a couple of issues. The fourth entry, *near-term milestones*, comes from managers' subschedules. Their subschedules may or not be contained in the project schedule in its entirety. Remember the approach suggested in Chapter 8, on planning, which involves planning milestones at the top level, while leaving the detail to the key manager's subschedules. Therefore, you want managers to talk about what is happening in the near term within their teams. You might (or might not) be amazed at how many disconnects I have uncovered through this process, as two mutually dependent teams may be working on different near-term milestones that have nothing to do with each other or on the same milestone with different end dates. There is no other way, short of creating a huge, unwieldy schedule, that you can capture all these details in the project schedule. Some data are needed, but discussion and communication are the best way to get the right issues out at the right time.

Figure 9-2: Key Manager's One-Pager

Requirement Changes:

- ➤ Schedule Tasks completed this week
- ➤ Schedule Tasks NOT completed this week (recovery plan for each)
- ➤ New tasks not previously planned
- ➤ Near term milestones: Planned   Actual   Risk
- ➤ Impediments to Success (Out of your control)

Finally, a few words on the last entry: *Impediments to success (out of your control)*. All the entries are important, of course, but this one is probably the most important. Many projects fail because team members are struggling with some aspect of their overall job scope but are afraid to ask for help. (See the pitfall "Pain-Avoiding Animals," discussed earlier in this chapter.) Used properly, this entry drives out that behavior. If you not only tell your teams that you want to know about issues they can't fix that are impacting them but also help to get them fixed, your credibility will go sky high.

For example, if a design tool runs at only 50 percent of the promised speed and one of your team members therefore can't simulate certain behavior modes of a circuit, the sooner you find out and get the team some help, the better. I have seen teams bury this kind of information for fear of being blamed or for fear of being driven to work 24/7 to deal with the problem, when by far the simplest (not easy by any means) solution is to get the tool vendor in to fix the problem.

Side Meetings

Ensure that your team understands that various meetings—such as all-hands and weekly team meetings—are key to your overall approach and the team's success and that they should both attend and participate in those meetings. This is because, left to their own devices and facing enormous performance pressure, they may be tempted to skip the wrong meetings: yours!

Also encourage them to have any side meetings needed to support the actions given in your team meetings or for their own reasons. Your team should have *any* additional meetings it thinks are necessary in order to do its jobs, while understanding that team members must also attend your key meetings.

Controlling Change Control

You cannot control knowledge workers. I don't even try. But go ahead, give it a try if you like. They almost certainly know more about their work than you do, so how are you going to control them? Get some data with which to beat them up? You know that won't work. Let's discuss change control from the viewpoint of Arun A., a successful practicing project manager in central Texas, and then we will look at two pitfalls with change control implications.

Arun says, "Change is a way of life. Anyone who says we will not make changes is not being truthful. Actually it is a planning process, just like any other planning process. So at my company we use a change committee. The most important part is prioritizing the changes based on what is really important versus nice to have versus desired."

Defining each of these levels is tricky, of course. And it is a multidimensional problem because there are different ways of looking at these levels depending on your viewpoint. "This is another source of communication breakdown in organizations," Arun says. For example, if a high-level manager from a customer discusses product features with a high-level person from the performing organization and says, "We would like to have that feature," what does that really mean? To a marketing VP, it sounds like "I must have this." To a design engineer, who is familiar with the target market from a different viewpoint, it might mean "nice to have."

So how to establish an effective change process? Arun says a consistent, robust change management process is key. "In my company we do this well. We get the right players together in a forum and we debate the priority of the changes. We may debate too much, actually, but we have people who represent the customer's side, and we work out what is really required." Arun's company, a major semiconductor company, takes a roadmap view. Sometimes this means that new features are delayed until a future release. In other words, the company looks at a market opportunity in an ongoing way, not as a single solution. It realizes that there is not time for the perfect part. For example, Arun says, "When you buy a house, you buy what you can afford. Then, later, you modify your home. If you needed everything in that house now, you could not afford it or wait for it to be built."

Arun's company also views change control as an organizational issue, not something done one-to-one by each designer with the design manager.

Arun believes that most problems with change control occur due to:

▶ Insufficient dialogue or communication up front in the cycle. Sometimes assumptions that are made early change later, and people forget to connect the dots.

▶ A failure to have the right players in the discussion.

▶ Changes in key team players, which leads to confusion resulting from recalibration by the new person or different viewpoints.

▶ Inherent misunderstandings resulting from imprecise language or simply, as Arun says, because "I saw a green elephant, and you saw a white elephant, but we each didn't know that."

Good change control occurs, then, when the right people get together in a trusting, periodic forum to communicate with integrity and passion what is best for the product. Sounds pretty TACTILE to me.

Project Pitfall: "That Schedule Buffer Is Mine!"

Good management technique says that every project must have a schedule buffer for unforeseen events. You could say that a cost buffer is needed, as well, but let's limit our discussion to schedule, as schedule is usually the number one focus in a technical development effort.

That means that your schedule may have a conclusion date of, say, April 15, while at the same time you are projecting that all work will be completed by February 15. The two months' difference is a schedule buffer, ostensibly to be judiciously used for various emergent issues.

I actually prefer to carry no schedule buffer, to be working to the conclusion date shown. Many people may find this naïve or foolish, but doing as I suggest avoids accusations that you have two sets of books and keeps the team focused on one overall goal.

But, in any case, who really owns the issue of end-date projection and buffer management? Sometimes management will do bizarre things around this issue, such as demanding that you do whatever is necessary to maintain a certain buffer, say two months, even as the project moves into final phases or encounters huge issues. The likely result will be hoarding of key information by your team as it pursues pain-avoiding behavior, which often ultimately results in major problems downstream.

Actions You Can Take

To be successful, you as project leader need to own the schedule buffer. Here are some ways to accomplish that:

▶ Have a clear process, approved beforehand by management, for how that buffer will be used and even if there will be one.

▶ Include a review of the buffer in every management review.

▶ Fight strongly against any "process" that artificially drives foolish behavior. For example, I once worked with a senior manager who forced the team to maintain a constant eight-week buffer no matter what occurred. Consequently the team was in constant replan mode, trying to find ways to refill the buffer that was being consumed for valid reasons.

Project Pitfall: Creepy Scope

Scope creep, as you no doubt know, is an insidious way for your project to get into trouble. It seems so innocuous: "This task was a bit more complicated that we thought it would be," or "Well, if we do that task that way, it means this whole set of tasks just got bigger." I understand that, but what can you do about it?

This problem should be minimal if you have been:

▶ Planning all tasks for the average time needed by an average employee, as mentioned in the section "Tool You Can Use: Project Planning Template," in Chapter 8. If you didn't do that in planning, at least plan new tasks that way and resolve to use this approach with your next project!

▶ Working hard to close the TBDs within the scope document, as mentioned in the section "Pre-Planning the Plan," in Chapter 7. If you didn't do so, at least ensure that you do so going forward and resolve to do so on your next project!

Actions You Can Take

What other proactive steps can you take?

▶ Ask probing questions anytime someone says, "We have to do this because of _____": (1) new task, (2) enlarged task, (3) all these things we now realize we must do because of numbers 1 and 2.

▶ Never initially say no to any request for new or enlarged work. Doing so will tend to polarize the discussion. Instead, your questions should create discussion concerning impacts in other areas of the team and whether there is an alternative way to get the same result without a hit to the schedule or the cost.

▶ Get your team of key project managers talking about and trying to solve these issues without assuming that scope creep is acceptable.

▶ If you assumed no schedule buffer, then you are free to argue that any new work necessarily will impact the end date of the affected milestone and the ultimate end date. Saying to your managers, "So, I am going to tell management we slipped the end date two weeks as a result of this new task, correct?" will inevitably focus the team on finding a joint work-around that doesn't slip the schedule. The next pitfall gets at this a bit more clearly.

Project Pitfall: Perfection Misdirection

Engineers and technical people tend to be smart, introverted, focused, and idealistic. None of that really gets us into much trouble in life. Oh, most technically trained people have stories similar to, "A bully in sixth grade ripped a corner of my favorite book," and that seems slightly traumatic. But we have one key personality trait in common that does cause problems on projects and in our lives.

Often we are perfectionists. As I frequently tell clients and team members, and even kids I coach in youth sports, perfection is unattainable. Perfection as a goal therefore is impossible to achieve. Making perfection your goal actually makes you less confident, since you can never achieve the goal. Perfectionists thus often have little self-confidence, even in the face of what are otherwise fine accomplishments. Perfection as a goal eventually leads a person to get cranky and brittle with others in a team, since they are part of what prevents him from being perfect.

Excellence is a much better goal. To be excellent means to be proud of (not arrogant about) what you are good at (your strengths) and to seek to use your talents to the maximum extent possible. Excellence also means understanding your weaknesses and creating a plan to continuously improve toward what you feel passion for, as you maximize your strengths and improve your weak areas so that they become increasingly less significant. To seek to be excellent in all we do implies balance in our lives.

As Ascension Health VP Marcia Silverberg says, "In my observation, many IT project managers aren't confident about their competence in the area of the soft skills, so they shy away from them. If they feel they can't do something well, especially with many of them being perfectionists, they may not even try, leading to all the sorts of problems in achieving project goals. We need to support IT project managers in learning and gaining confidence in their 'soft skills' for maximum project effectiveness."

Actions You Can Take

These actions will help you avoid perfection misdirection:

► This sounds like soft stuff, but try it anyway: Talk— early and often—about the difference between perfection and excellence. Make sure your team understands that their goal is *excellence*.

► Do simple exercises with your team, such as having members all take and discuss as a team the assessment in *Strengthfinders 2.0* (Gallup Press, 2007), by Tom Rath. During the discussion, emphasize that technical people tend to have analytical strengths that they unknowingly overuse and how the overuse of those strengths can lead to perfectionism.

Selling New Baselines

Effective change control, along with clever tweaking of your milestones, is meant to allow you to deal with small changes along the way without violating agreed-to project goals for schedule and cost. But almost inevitably there will be a change so major that a new baseline involving changes to the schedule, cost, and scope will be necessary. Then what?

Proceed carefully. The reaction by management and customers to such a pronouncement on your part can vary widely. You have to judge before you say anything about what those reactions are likely to be and how to best deal with them. And you have to be right.

Although I would like to say, as demonstrated by the "Three Letter Agency" situation described in Chapter 4, that honesty is always the best policy, it just isn't that simple. As Larry's story in Chapter 5 shows, there are too many variables to manage with just one approach.

You have to follow your key internal guidelines. My view of integrity drives me to confront problems. I may overuse this strength at times, but my first action would be to come up with a desired course of action, then discuss the situation with a trusted senior person. Ideally, this would be my immediate supervisor. Try to find common ground in this and all subsequent conversations. You don't want the supervisor to think getting rid of you is the easiest way to deal with the problem.

I would flexibly apply my integrity. Don't be a complete hardhead here. Life is not strictly black and white. And don't be cynical; this is not my way of saying, "Get along by going along." Instead, see if, like James in Chapter 4, you can get support from your management chain to simply tell the customer the truth and then do the replan that is needed. If not, find a solution that works within your integrity. If you can't make that happen, think about looking for a new position. You will live to regret hiding a major problem in the hopes that it will go away. You were hired not to hide problems but rather to find the best way to solve them. And, remember, the best way is not always perfect.

Bring others as needed into the problem resolution. You will need all your hard-earned, stored-up trust from your team leaders, your team in general, and management. Create a stand-alone new plan that can be clearly scrutinized for the baseline schedule, cost, scope, and risk impacts.

Once you have a plan that seems the best blend of all the involved interests, move on to a discussion with your customer. Be like James here. He was honest and direct and offered options. Let others vent their emotions; then engage their intellects. Do not respond in kind to emotional outbursts. Also, never argue with fools; people around you may not be able to tell who the fool is.

Once the new work is agreed to, blend it into the existing schedule, cost, scope, and risk reporting. But always have a way to separate the new work from the baseline so that people can see your plan for the new effort and later can measure how you performed.

Learning How to Win

You've made it to the end game, the last quarter or so of the project. Of course, there have been a few bumps along the way, but you are making it happen.

You feel great! You've hit all your milestones so far. Sure, maybe you had to move a little work from one milestone to the next, but everything held together. The team is working well, raising and solving problems *together*. Your customer is happy with what she sees. Your management food chain can see that it is going to have a new capability or product to sell soon. You've gotten into position to win. Now you have to learn how to close, to finish successfully.

To do so requires a different mindset, a more focused and more detailed approach. "Wait," you say. "This approach was working! I'm going to ride the horse that got me here! I'm going to dance with the person that brought me to the party!"

I understand your concern, so let's try a few analogies. In sports, as in business, we see large groups of people under pressure to perform difficult tasks that can take a long time. I find these analogies to be effective with teams if presented in the right context and not overdone.

▶ A cross-country runner does not use the same strategy in the first mile as she will toward the end of her race. She may be content to hang back in the middle of the pack in the beginning, masking her true capabilities and saving enough energy for a *kick*, a burst of speed at the end of the race that will carry her to victory.

▶ A football coach, along with his staff, creates a complicated game plan before the contest. One standard game plan is to run the football—that is, to pound the ball on the ground—until the defense is worn down a bit, then move to an offense that primarily passes the ball, taking advantage of the opponent's tendency to bunch near the line, allowing the offense's swift receivers to run right past them.

But I have found that the analogy that works best with knowledge worker managers and teams is not about the sports in this list but rather about baseball. You may, of course, find none of these analogies useful with your teams. I wish I knew more about cricket and lacrosse!

Tool You Can Use: Seventh-Inning Beginning

A baseball manager makes myriad decisions, large and small, throughout the course of a nine-inning baseball game. But he doesn't manage the same way throughout the game. Early in the game, he may change little in his approach, content to see how his team is playing to his plan. In contrast, toward the end of the game, he may make changes such as using different pitchers, pinch (substitute) hitters, and pinch runners frequently—even between pitches—because he recognizes that the end game requires a different focus.

The Seventh Inning Beginning tool, shown in Figure 9-3, allows you to manage differently as your project enters the final stretch. Each functional or key manager should fill out a copy of Figure 9-3. Managing like this is tiring for you, your managers, and your team. Exactly when you should switch to this approach depends on your peculiar set of circumstances. For projects of roughly a year or less, my rule of thumb is that the last six to eight weeks might be managed like this. For longer projects, three months might be optimal. Note that this is not a cookbook or a precise formula that must be adhered to exactly. Before we look in detail at the tool itself, here is a set of guidelines to which you should apply appropriate situational judgment.

▶ **Expanded Schedule:** Your schedule needs to be expanded at this point, to ensure that the interconnections between functions are crystal clear. Add any new major milestones needed, although, as you have been doing this all along, there are likely to be few. Each functional manager should add detail to his or her subschedules, and there should be a short team meeting to combine them, similar to how the top-level schedule was done in planning. The schedule will now become a detailed day-to-day schedule, with additional detail added as you move forward, always keeping roughly the next two weeks (or key milestone) planned at the day-to-day level.

▶ **Risk List:** Each major milestone needs a list of risks and a SMART plan for minimizing that risk. The risk avoidance plans for the next few milestones should be discussed briefly at every team meeting.

▶ **Cost:** You should relax cost as a constraint at this point. This is because any short-term costs required to keep you on schedule are likely to be relatively small compared with the impact of missing your market window. Why waste much time analyzing and justifying additional cost at this point? Of course, if that assumption is wrong for your circumstances, tailor your approach.

▶ **Scope:** Change control is critical in the final portion of the project. As you approach your deadline, you need a small change control board. I recommend you have three people: the design manager (or leading technical team member), yourself, and the biggest picture person on the team, perhaps the integration manager if you have one. The entire functional staff should have input, but not a final vote. Narrowing down the number of decision makers will ensure that there are fewer change requests and a quicker resolution.

➤ **War Room:** You need to commandeer the use of an area with walls and a door for the duration of the project. Small conference rooms serve nicely. This *war room* is a place where you can leave detailed schedules and risk lists on the wall for all to see. The room should stay unlocked so that team members can drop by to look at the wall contents. This should not become your office for the duration, only a place where the team meets to discuss the remainder of the project. Optimally, daily stand-up meetings are the only meetings that should occur here. This will encourage an atmosphere of *doing* around the meetings.

➤ **The tool itself:** The Seventh Inning Beginning tool (see Figure 9-3) is a snapshot of what your team needs to focus on that day. You should update the data shown real-time at each meeting and both post the results on the war room wall and send them to each team member immediately after the daily war room meetings. Your main focus needs to be on the tasks and risks and the actions needed to avert those risks for the next few milestones. That takes up the bulk of the page. Next, list all the remaining milestones. At the bottom of the page are entries for Work Days Remaining to Project Completion, Scheduled Completion, and a calculation of the remaining buffer. Your schedule should be detailed enough at this point to allow you to see how many days of work remain. I do not believe detailed buffer management makes much sense until roughly the final quarter of the project (now). If you and the team have done a good job, you will likely have a buffer (not manufactured or manipulated) at this point. If this buffer begins to shrink, obviously this needs to be discussed and action plans undertaken to stop the shrinkage.

➤ **Team Meetings:** Your team should meet as often as needed—daily most of the time—in the war room for fifteen-minute stand-up meetings. The meeting agenda should include a quick look at the next few days, using the tool to facilitate the sharing of information on what each person is doing that day and needs from

Figure 9-3: The 7th Inning Beginning Tool

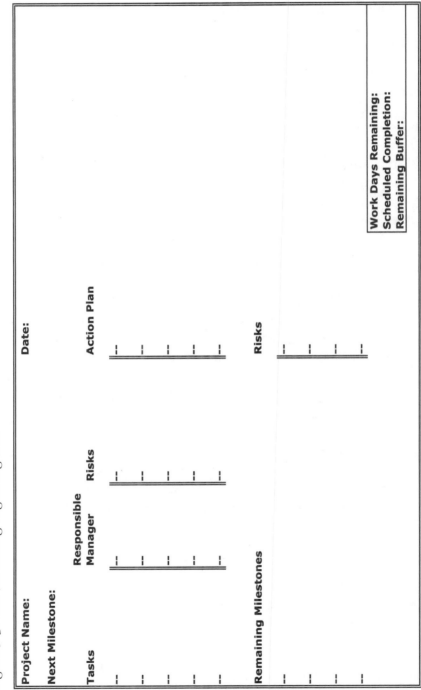

others, and what they need to finish a task that is due soon. I mean it when I say that these meetings should take no more than fifteen minutes.

Project Pitfall: Done vs. Done-Done

After months of hard work on a project, enjoying many small successes (and maybe some minor failures), meeting milestones and achieving internal goals, how do you finally declare victory? So far, you and your team have done a good job in planning; you have dealt with the potential pitfalls along the way. You have had to replan a little, but now you're almost done, and you can almost smell victory. But what does *done* really mean? Many times I hear technical people, in response to a statement from someone who says, "I'm done," reply by saying, "Yes, but are you *done-done?*"

What, pray tell, does that mean? Aren't we either done or not? Not in the world of perfectionist engineers. *Done* may mean any of a number of things, ranging from thorough overdoneness to sloppy inadequacy.

The problem here is the defining of exit criteria. Technical people who don't have clear exit criteria may worry excessively that they didn't do everything necessary to do the task well. Unmonitored, this behavior may result in what euphemistically is called "boiling the ocean," or something even more colorful. If this behavior is left unchecked until the end of the project, you will have resources hanging around costing money, potentially breaking things, and not moving on to new projects that need them.

Actions You Can Take

To get to *done-done* on your project:

▶ You must have clear exit criteria for those technical requirements that define acceptability from the customer's and the end user's points of view.

▶ To develop these criteria, devote some of your team meeting to the topic and develop a team approach that works.

➤   Also have the team member's work together as appropriate to clarify what constitutes acceptance criteria for each of the requirements. Just approach this as a commonsense exercise, not as a big engineering project, and you will be fine. Communication by the right people is key.

Case Study: The Path Less Taken

It is during the executing phase that your good approach and planning should come together in a series of successful accomplishments. You can certainly see that that is the case in Sheila's TACTILE section presented here, but not so much for Ravi in the Standard approach, in spite of his hard work and his many years with BTC.

Standard Approach

Ravi's lack of cohesive team leadership ability begins to manifest in a multitude of ways. He simply isn't able to manage technical problems *through* people.

Executing to the Plan

Month 6 of Planned Eighteen-Month Project
Team Meeting

"We've been through this," Bennett (never Ben) says, so frustrated that he is almost shouting at Lance. "There isn't time to do it."

"Then we have to make time. Have your people work more hours. I don't see them all in here at midnight like my guys when I make my last run-through for the night."

"What!" Now Bennett is really angry. "They work their tails off. We all do. The problem is the rookies in your shop—"

"Guys, guys," Ravi says. "That is enough; enough tearing each other apart. As Lance says, there is no extra time. We cannot take from the schedule buffer, and so we will have to just work more hours to make our code freeze milestone. Maybe in a couple of places I can add headcount, but that is it."

Ravi looks around the room. Half the people are writing e-mails, not even listening closely. The others appear ready for open warfare. He sighs. "Let's move on."

Rajesh mutters to Zev, "Code freeze, huh. Code *slush* more like it." Zev nods heavily.

Controlling Change Control

Month 9 of Planned Eighteen-Month Project
Key Managers' Team Meeting

"I *can't* change it now," Tom Thompson, the layout manager, says as calmly as he can. "The assumptions that drove that decision were made weeks or months ago."

"I would have two more months of new work, Bennett, if we do as you suggest," adds Zev Cohen, the verification manager.

Bennett doesn't react. "Has to be done." He looks at Ravi. "Not my fault that Lance was working to rev AB on the SCRED when everyone else was on AC. I can't help it that Tom was too cautious three months ago. And, Zev, that's your problem. You verify what we design. The change has to be made. All there is to it."

Ravi sighs. "Leanne, what impact will there be to the schedule if we do as Bennett suggests?"

Leanne has been pushing buttons frantically since Bennett first introduced the issue. She looks up at Ravi, mild panic on her face. "I don't know, two months maybe. Less with ten more people."

"Two months!" Bennett scoffs. "You guys just need to get it done. Ravi, you have been here longer than most of the rest of us. We just suck it up and make it happen, right?"

All eyes are on Ravi as he nods. "We do not have two months to take from the buffer. Deborah watches that like a hawk. Perhaps Leanne and I can find two weeks somehow without touching the buffer. Everyone just fix this and say nothing about it. None of us need to be in Deborah's office an hour each day explaining ourselves."

Selling New Baselines

Month 12 of Planned Eighteen-Month Project

Executive VP and CTO Deborah Tabor's Office, BTC Main Tower, 3:00 P.M.

As he walks in, Ravi surveys the scene. Deborah's rather large conference room is crowded. They are all there, as he knew they would be. Mark Simpson and his entire staff are there, including Ravi's boss, Sebastian. Ravi's key project functional managers are present, arrayed in one long line as if to be used for quick target practice. And several people he doesn't recognize are present. *Uh-oh*, he thinks. Beside him he hears Leanne make a strange sound, part strangling, part snuffling. Before he can speak, Deborah says with a smile, "Ravi, what is this we hear about your project having problems?"

He hitches his pants up and speaks. "Good morning, everyone." He glances at Deborah. "Yes, we have found a problem in some of the verification runs. This by itself is, of course, not so unusual—"

Deborah turns to Zev Cohen, the Alpha Omega verification manager. "Zev, how can this be?" Zev looks levelly at her but says nothing.

Ravi continues. "As I said, problems in verification—"

"What kind of problems, Ravi? Verification by its nature finds problems. How can you have problems with verification? Did Zev not do his job? This I find hard to believe. Perhaps this is masking something else?"

Ravi stops. "Deborah, we have problems across the board, but verification testing missed some things that were confused coming from the design team."

"What kind of explanation is this?"

Ravi gathers himself and looks right at Deborah. "I am trying to describe a complicated set of issues. If you would just let me explain it, perhaps it would make more sense."

Deborah smiles tightly at him. "By all means, Ravi. Please go ahead. Please *explain*."

Two hours later...
Same Meeting

Deborah stands and approaches the front of the room. "This project, Alpha Omega, is simply too important to fail. If we slip two months, as Ravi finally told us, we will miss the key selling season for our customers. You know our cycle times in the factory will not make up for a big design slip." She looks around the room. "You all had a chance to say what you had to say. Are we all agreed on our action?" She sees general nodding.

"Then we will have daily meetings here at 6:00 P.M. I will have to shuffle some meetings. If I am not here for some reason, you have the meeting anyway. I will try to be here. Sebastian, you, of course, will be here." She looks at Mark Simpson. "And, of course, Mark, whoever else you want." She looks at Ravi. "I will get a schedule from Ravi and . . ." She looks at Leanne. "Leanne is your name, yes?"

Leanne nods quickly.

"And we will take four weeks of the eight remaining weeks of buffer. We cannot afford to take more. Leanne, you can do this in APS?" Leanne nods again.

Deborah looks at Ravi and around the room at each functional manager on Ravi's team. "You all know what is required. Whatever it takes to get this project done so that we hit our window. I have done this many times myself. Your families will understand. It is the price for working at the best technology company in the world. If you cannot do this, come see me after this and we will find you something else to do. Maybe it will not be here, I do not know. But I think you know I am serious. Failure is not an option."

No one says a word as the meeting adjourns.

Learning How to Win

Month 20 of Planned Eighteen-Month Project
Project Team Meeting
Tilapia Conference Room, 10:30 P.M.

Ravi stands in exhausted triumph. "Then we are agreed. This is all we can do. A 10 percent final hit to frequency, some of which will be made up by bin selection. Yes?"

Wearily, they all nod.

Ravi smiles. "All of your hard work is now worth it as we go kick Intel and AMD's behinds."

More weary nods as they file out of the conference room.

Zev looks over at Jiao Lee, the design assurance manager. "Going home?"

Jiao smiles. "Home? I may just go back to my cubicle and take a nap."

TACTILE Approach

Sheila has built trust with her team and management, and the results show it during the critically important execution phase.

Executing to the Plan

Month 6 of Planned Eighteen-Month Project
Key Managers' Team Meeting
Steeleye Salmon Conference Room

All eyes are on Sheila. Only one person, Rajesh, is doing e-mail and he quickly finishes and closes his laptop.

"Let's get started," Sheila says. "Here's the milestone list. As you can see, we have successfully completed the first twelve milestones on time, to the day. Good job for that. We will have pizza for everyone in Mahi Mahi conference room on Friday from eleven to one." She looks around. "Where's Scott? Or should we go ahead with your one-pagers?"

At that instant, Scott Williams, her program manager, rushes in. "I just sent the latest earned value report," he says. "I can project it or you can, doesn't matter, it's all good." He joins the people in the room in a big grin.

Thirty minutes later...
Same Meeting

Sheila raises her hand. "Lance. Just a second." She glances over at Jiao Lee, her design assurance manager. "Jiao, how does what Lance just said affect you?"

"Yes, thank you," Jiao replies. "I was just thinking that the Pericles tool, as it is, would not do this."

Lance frowns. "I didn't know that. I asked Max at lunch last week about this."

Jiao smiles. "Max works for the vendor. You should ask me."

"How about you two settle this in a side meeting?" Sheila interjects. "Is that it for you, Lance?"

Later that week …

Division Staff Meeting

Mark Simpson's Conference Room

"Too much good news," says Sanjay Singh, the division financial controller.

"Is this really possible, all milestones on time to date with no problems?" says Deborah Tabor, the division chief technology officer (CTO).

Sheila smiles from the podium. "The team has had many problems, Deborah. Just none that cost us schedule and none that got to this forum."

"This I like, Sheila," Deborah says with a smile.

"Sounds like the schedule was too easy to start with," replies Singh.

Sheila looks at T.J. Anderson, the division marketing VP, for comment. "Nope," T.J. says. "If they continue, we will make the market window easy." She pauses. "Well, not easy, but I assumed a couple of months of problems when I gave Sheila the date. She's doing great."

Sheila smiles at them from the podium. "Shall we go on to the next slide?" she asks.

Controlling Change Control

Month 12 of Planned Eighteen-Month Project

Change Control Board Meeting

Mississippi Mudcat Conference Room

"So requirement 2.2.3.1.2 is changed to 'frequency shall be 3.2Ghz +/-5%.' Is that correct, Bennett?" Scott Williams, Sheila's PM, asks.

"Correct."

"And everyone else agrees that this has no overall impact on anyone's schedule? Jiao, Mira, Lance, Zev, Tom, Rajesh?"

They all answer affirmatively, only Zev holding back just a bit.

"Sheila," Scott says, "looks like the change control meeting is done for today. And early, I might add."

Selling New Baselines

Month 12 of Planned Eighteen-Month Project
CTO Deborah Tabor's Conference Room

Sheila is getting a little hot under the collar, but as of yet it isn't showing on the outside. She consciously slows her breathing. "As I said, Deborah, this is the complete cost and task breakdown. There is no confusion or mixing with what is here and the existing baseline. Nothing here has changed since I sent the slides out on Monday."

"Yes, Sheila. I hear you." Deborah smiles at her bemusedly. "How can you be so sure this is all there is? SCRED is a difficult piece of new work, no?"

"SCRED is hard, it's true. Hard to do, hard to estimate. I am *sure* because I trust the team."

"I see. Trust." Deborah pauses. "Trust, but who verified? Zev?" There is light laughter at the joke.

Sheila replies carefully. "Deborah, we took a fair amount of time, working some pretty late hours together to make sure we had it right. We stand behind it. Unless there are more questions, are we approved?"

Deborah looks at each member of Sheila's functional manager team, arrayed around the room. All she sees is certainty. "A project whose functional managers agree on something around here? Surely this cannot be." She pauses. "I, for one, agree," Deborah finally says with a small smile.

Learning How to Win

Month 18 of Planned Eighteen-Month Project
Crappy Conference/War Room, 8:15 A.M.

"I think that is the right list of tests," Zev says.

"For done, or *done-done*?" Sheila asks.

Zev looks quizzically at her. "*Done-done*, Sheila. Isn't that the only way we do things?"

Sheila nods, then looks around. "Any other issues before we get out of here and go finish this thing?"

They all grin as they leave the team's war room.

TACTILE Analysis

By now, we see the benefits of Sheila's TACTILE approach. While Ravi is struggling with his team and with his management—most clearly demonstrated by the scene with CTO Deborah Tabor—Sheila has a highly functioning team, and her reviews with management go well.

▶ **Transparency:** Sheila's reviews with management go so well because she is transparent in her actions. All of her stakeholders see this, and it reflects in the culture of all her interactions.

▶ **Accountability:** The first two scenes in the standard section demonstrate that Ravi has not created an accountability culture. In the first scene, Bennett and Lance get into a shouting match instead of being led by Ravi to focus on the issue that needed resolving. In the second scene, Ravi allows Bennett to drive the team in a direction that ultimately places Ravi in the hot seat with Deborah in a future scene. On the other hand, Sheila is shown holding the team accountable for working together on the Pericles tool issue when she asks Jiao Lee how an issue raised by Lance affects Jiao. This process of simple questions is easy to use and works just like this in the real world.

▶ **Communication:** The communication channel around Ravi is strained; every conversation has negative undertones. People get their jobs done, but they struggle with each other. Sheila does not have to struggle like Ravi because she has created the right culture.

▶ **Trust:** There is little trust on the standard project, while the TACTILE project is successful because people trust one another and what they hear. This is especially true for management, which trusts what it hears from Sheila.

▶ **Integrity:** Ravi misses a chance to demonstrate integrity when he tries to hide the rev level difference, implying in the meeting with Deborah that Zev is to blame. Sheila, in contrast, sees that problems get worked out as needed in a business-like way, letting her integrity speak for itself.

▶ **Leadership:** Ravi and his team work hard, but his leadership adds little. Leadership is Sheila's greatest strength.

▶ **Execution Results:** Ravi is late, and his team feels beat up. It also does not meet some of the performance requirements. Actually, these are not bad results for a standard project. But Sheila's team stays on track throughout the project and is not exhausted at the finish, a much better result.

We've now learned how the TACTILE approach works in initiating, planning, and executing. You've gotten some useful tips and techniques to help you manage those three critical phases of your project.

In the next chapter, we discuss monitoring, controlling, and reporting of the key information you need to ensure success during the project. Too often, people view monitor and control as removed from the team's project responsibilities, perhaps even done by a separate finance or project controls group. This may not be the sexiest part of the project, but don't take your eyes off the prize yet—you're almost home, and getting the next phase right is critical to finding your way.

CHAPTER 10

Monitoring, Controlling, and Reporting

MONITORING AND CONTROLLING seems boring. After all, careers aren't made in monitoring and controlling—they are made in execution—but they can be lost here. The dictionary definition might be "regularly observing project execution and measuring variances to plan so that appropriate corrective actions can occur." My view is that monitoring and controlling are about correctly deciding what limited set of data you need and how to effectively adjust based on what those data show you. I have added reporting as a separate entry because how and what you report is at least as important as the data you collect and the actions you take to control your project.

Frankly, there is often an overly analytical, impersonal feel to how this project phase is approached in the PM profession. PMs are too often trained to bother anybody on the project until they get the data they think they need to control the project. Then they try to implement their decisions and often find they don't get the cooperation to make it work.

Your job is to *work with* (not control) your stakeholders—management, customer, and team—within a disciplined framework to drive the right business results. A little bit of control goes a long way. There are three areas to get right:

1. Monitoring
2. (Don't Even Try to) Control
3. Reporting

Monitoring

Much of what the *PMBOK Guide* would have you do to monitor we did in an integrated way in execution, as discussed in Chapter 9. How you report on the data is much more political than what data you gather. Therefore, monitoring is a much simpler situation than we find with controlling and reporting. You just need to gather the data you need to manage your project successfully. No more, no less.

A Better Approach

How do you determine what needs to be monitored? Arun A., our post-silicon test manager for a major technology company in Austin, says, "If something is quantifiable, it can be controlled." Arun monitors the feature-level criteria that he is responsible for testing. He translates his quality standards for each feature into exit criteria and has bands that show how close he is to the exit criteria. Arun recommends that the project manager adopt a similar approach, based on the project exit criteria, such as "Did I meet all interface specifications, or ESD standards, SPC compliance, and so forth?"

The data needed to establish the exit criteria are not what you or management think are needed to watch your team and you closely but are rather what you and the team need to enable success. The data should be quantifiable, of course, but there is a different emphasis here, on trust building, accountability, communication, and transparency. You all work for the same organization, after all. Why shouldn't you learn to trust and work with one another?

You should have started this process early by talking about what data you needed with your key managers during planning. Then, during execution, you should have been using the data you collected to provide actions that the team could use to generate the desired business results. In this way, monitoring is integrated with your execution effort, rather than being a stand-alone pain-in-the-neck of extra work.

Project Pitfall: "You Know These People Can't Be Trusted, Don't You?"

More than one senior manager has said to me the exact words I used in the heading to this section. Famous last words they are. If you believe this about any team you are leading, you will likely not succeed.

Your company—if it is anything like the fine companies I have worked for—expends a lot of effort to hire the very best people for the important development projects that it undertakes. Then the people come on board, and immediately they are viewed as untrustworthy. The solution? A whole bunch of extra metrics to generate data with which to catch them acting in an untrustworthy fashion and then whack them over the head.

If your team is acting in an untrustworthy manner, it is your issue to resolve. You create and own the project culture. I will bet you a lunch at Z Tejas, a well-known lunch hangout in Austin, that your team is composed of people who, if led properly, are just dying to act in a trustworthy manner. At least, that has been my experience when I have approached teams with the right attitude.

Yet, often, when I have spoken this way, the response has been scorn or verbal derision. I was once told, "We canceled a large, very important project because we found out these people were not telling the truth about status and in some cases even changed the data! This next project [which I was on] is going to have enough metrics to make sure those people can't cheat."

Hmm. To me, it seems far easier to create an environment where they don't feel the need to lie. Sure, there may be a few bad apples in the barrel that need to be reassigned or shown the door, but, when confronted with statements like these, I ask questions, such as "What happened when someone brought up a problem?" Usual answer: "We jumped right on it." Interpretation: "We jumped right on *them*."

Another question: "What do you do when they ask for help?" Usual answer: a quizzical look followed by "They don't ask for help. We make sure our teams handle their own problems." Interpretation: "They better not ask for help. We hired them to solve problems. If they need help, why do we need them?"

Actions You Can Take

These actions can help you create a culture of trust on your team:

▶   Tell team members that you trust them and act trustworthy yourself. This in itself will be an enormous change in most organizations and will create a better working atmosphere almost immediately.

▶   When problems occur, do not assume you are being lied to. Instead, probe for the bottom-line problem—find out what is *really* happening. Craft a solution that incorporates what is best for the business, the team, and the individuals involved. If solutions for those three groups are mutually exclusive, you must do what is best for the organization, but I can't think of very many times when the choice was that stark.

▶   If you find you have been lied to, do the following: stop trusting the person. Tell him he let down you, himself, and the team. If you can get him removed from your team, do so. If he is too valuable or politically connected for that, at least have a serious discussion with his supervisor and get it noted on his yearly performance review if you can. I have never had to go this far in my career. Any interactions along these lines ended before I got to that extreme.

Project Pitfall: "The Data Are There! Let's Use Them!"

The following has actually happened to me twice during my career, at two different companies. Engineering, Finance, or some organization will have some sort of performance data in a database that has been collected for who knows what purpose. The data appear to be convertible to some metric or metrics that could conceivably have some value to someone (not you or your team) interested in how your team is doing.

Some powerful person in management will suggest in an excited tone of voice: "Did you know these data were there? What wonderful things we can see with these data! We can slice and dice them a thousand ways from Sunday to see how you are doing. Isn't that great?"

No. It is *not* great. It is an absolute nightmare. The data are not always clean or readily convertible to beneficial use. I have seen data like these used to form contradictory conclusions about what needs to be done and long arguments ensue that waste a lot of time and energy.

Actions You Can Take

Assuming that you have a system (similar to what has been outlined throughout this book) that works for your project, you can resist this pitfall.

▶ Use the ROI argument to support why you don't want to mess with the data. That is: "We didn't budget for the effort. We don't have resources to divert to that effort, and the data we currently have are working fine for what we need."

▶ If all else fails, have someone experiment with the data conversion away from your project personnel, and report on that effort separately from your normal reporting.

Controlling (Don't Even Try)

First, disabuse yourself of the idea that you can control anything. As author Tom Kendrick says in his book *Results without Authority*

(AMACOM, 2006), "In classes, workshops, and informal discussions of project management that I've been a part of, one of the most common questions is always, 'How can I manage my project if I have no power or authority?'" These folks are articulating a concern about lack of control. They know they are nominally in charge, but they don't know how to lead, how to create results through people.

Their mistake is in thinking that their job is somehow to control. Intuitively, you know this is true if you have ever had a one-year-old child in your house, and one-year-olds are relatively defenseless. They are good on offense, but their defense is weak.

So why would you think it is possible to control a modern IT or development project, with your diverse management food chain, hundreds of team members, and customers who often aren't even sure what they really want? You control nothing. Say it loud and say it proud: "I control NADA, nothing, zip, zero."

Standard Control Systems

A multitude of project management systems have evolved over the years to cover schedule and cost estimating, risk management, scope management, configuration management, quality management, and so forth. There is a tendency to think that merging all these diverse systems into one central project database, often called Project Management Information Systems (PMIS), is a good thing. And these tools, like any good tool, have their place on our projects.

But there is an overreliance in the project management community on PMIS. The *PMBOK Guide* defines PMIS as "an automated system used by the project management team to aid execution of the activities planned in the project management plan." This sounds fairly innocuous, but there are a few areas to watch out for. First, the automated nature of these systems means that the output is only as good as the original input and the frequency and the accuracy of the updating. Second, they are fairly expensive and thus can drive out other worthy uses of resources. Third, these systems are often viewed as all-knowing Delphic oracles, where project teams are driven to be subservient to the data as opposed to solving real emerging problems.

My approach does not require the use of PMIS, but using them is fine, as long as you keep in mind the three constraints described earlier. After all, the proper use of any tool is only to supply information that can help solve problems.

A Better Approach

Okay, okay. I know we have to control in the sense of making changes based on data, as in a feedback control system. But distributed, not central, control is the way to go. The central planning way is to have an army of people gather data, create metrics, and tell people what to do on the basis of conclusions drawn by you and that army of people. The distributed way is to work everything through your team of key managers, as they should in turn work through their team members. This requires no small army of data gatherers and creates a better team culture. In either case, you may use a PMIS. This is not about systems or tools as much as it is about how you use the data.

If you do this right, your team will trust you and consequently follow your lead with more commitment and better results. Yes, you need some metrics to see how things are going and to help predict where you are headed. I believe capturing the output of those metrics in a project leader's one-page scorecard is the right approach, as we discuss in the next few pages.

If you try to control rather than trusting your team, you will have dissension and passive-aggressive behavior. The following actions will combat this:

► All performance feedback to the team should be reported to the key managers first, in your team meetings.

► You should give the overview of the project's performance at every weekly team meeting. Do not cede that role to anyone.

► The key managers should report on their own progress.

► Problems, potential (risks) or real, that require even a slight change to the baseline schedule, cost, or scope plans or to the top-level risk register should be discussed with the key managers and a team decision made. Of course, your role is leading the team to the right decision.

➤   You should never make a change to the project arbitrarily with just one of the managers. You have no idea what impact seemingly small decisions can have on other subteams. And such an action will drive a wedge into your efforts to get the key managers to work together.

Stoplight Charts

Most project managers in my experience either use too few or too many metrics to try to understand their projects. Use too few and you run the risk of missing things. Use too many and you run the risk of confusing yourself and others, as well as burning a lot of person power in the effort. We mentioned earlier that Arun A. keeps a scorecard of the key functional requirements he is responsible for testing. He uses a standard Red-Yellow-Green scorecard approach—what is commonly called a stoplight chart—with preset +/– percentage triggers for each color. For example, if the variance to the requirement is greater than 20 percent, the stoplight for that requirement might be red. If the variance is less than 20 percent but greater than 10 percent, the color might be yellow. If the variance is less than 10 percent, the color may be green.

I have seen the stoplight concept used often. Smarter Solutions in Austin, Texas, even has what it calls the Integrated Enterprise Excellence System, which does a very sophisticated version of this with organizational level metrics.

Project Pitfall: "Does That Weigh Enough?"

Mike S. in New Mexico once created an entire project management plan that was organized in a stoplight chart manner. Mike wanted to be efficient, with both time and prose, so he constructed his project management plan as mostly a collection of tables of requirements, using the following criteria as a control mechanism: less than 5 percent variance, the PM owns the issue (green); 5 to

10 percent, management gets involved in solving (yellow); greater than 10 percent, customer is notified (red). This resulted in what Mike considered to be an excellent example of a project management plan. His manager, used to doing things a certain way, had clear ideas on what was involved in a project management plan and rejected Mike's plan with the words "Does this thing really weigh enough?"

Mike had to battle management expectations and at the same time deal with control issues, showing the interconnectedness of these concepts. Because of this, his effort could also be considered a function of planning.

Actions You Can Take

Mike took an innovative approach to the creation of his project management plan, but his effort to be clear and concise failed because he didn't place himself in his manager's mindset.

▶ What could Mike have done differently? "I should have gone to him ahead of time and asked the simple question 'Are there any length requirements?'" Mike says wryly, another way of saying that he should have discovered his supervisor's expectations.

▶ Socialize your intentions properly when trying to do something innovative or different from the norm in the culture you find yourself in. But don't overcommunicate either, as that can confuse people and create false resistance due to unfounded fears. This can bog you down.

Tool You Can Use: Project Manager's One-Pager

You should have a list of key project metrics organized as a stoplight chart. The Project Manager's One-Pager (see Figure 10-1) is by no means the only way you can do this. The key takeaway here is that you should monitor those metrics that are important to you and thus your ability to create the desired business results. I prefer to limit the number of key metrics that are constantly tracked to about ten. I have seen stoplight charts with thirty or more entries—

Figure 10-1: Project Manager's One-Pager

Project Name:	Pegasus Rider						Date:		11/5/2006			
Project Manager:	Doug Russell											

	Plan	Jan	Feb	Mar	Apr	May	Jun	Jul	Aug	Sep	Oct	Nov	Dec
Contract Summary													
Customer Metrics													
Perception													
Deliverables Status													
Emergent Issues													
Management Metrics													
Quality Summary													
Schedule / Cost to Goal													
Top 10 Risk Status Change													
Procurement Issues													
Team Metrics													
Space													
Labor Hours vs. Plan													
% Unresolved Problem													

far too many. Of course, there may be other information that you look at as needed.

As you can see, the one-pager is organized into three main areas: customer, management, and team metrics.

The key guidelines of your metrics are as follows:

▶   Each of the three areas has no more than three or four key metrics, which should be matched to the expectations of your customer, management, and team. My list is just a guideline; you should create a list of key metrics that work for you.

▶   Since you have so few metrics, they all must be well thought out and count for something. For example, you cannot tolerate a red condition for a metric for twelve straight months, as I saw on one project stoplight chart for, of all things, a Quality 5 Up metric.

▶   Any metric that is red for two consecutive months should drive some management engagement in a sincere, effective way to *help* you.

▶   Every metric should have explicit rules for green, yellow, and red status. They should not be amorphous qualitative measures.

▶   Each metric that is in a yellow or red state should have an associated SMART action plan.

▶   You may redefine red or yellow criteria only in the most transparent way with all involved parties. Redefining criteria is generally a bad idea because people will be tempted to redefine their way out of trouble, but this is better than carrying a metric as red for twelve months.

▶   There may be some filtering or selecting of which data to show, but the same data set should be used in all forums and with all stakeholders.

My choices for the top ten metrics are described next.

Customer Metrics

Customer metrics are the hardest metrics to make both quantitative and simple, but you should work hard to find a way to report on soft issues concerning your customer because—done well—they can serve as great leading indicators of potential future business relationship problems.

▶ **Customer Perception:** Is the customer upset enough to complain to your management? If so, your project isn't green. Don't know? Then ask. That will build trust and a better long-term relationship. But don't be so harsh on yourself that you wind up automatically in a nongreen status. If the customer is likely to complain about even one substantive issue (i.e., related to the schedule, cost, or performance requirements of the project or related to your relationship with the customer), then score this yellow. If the issue goes unresolved for a second month, score it red. You should not carry any issue longer than two months with excuses like "You know Katherine is still upset about that old issue, so it's still red." That old issue should have been resolved to Katherine's satisfaction by now!

▶ **Deliverables Status:** You have a list of deliverables to the customer. Are any of them late? If so, you are yellow. As earlier, if any of the deliverables are late for two straight months, then you are red. Obviously, this makes no sense if you are building hundreds of some piece of hardware and one of them was shipped late. Use percentage bands for yellow and red criteria in those cases.

▶ **Emergent Issues:** Not all metrics should look backward. Here is your opportunity to show your risk avoidance ability. Is there anything on your project that is likely to emerge as an issue that will cause complaint or will cause a deliverable to be late in the future? Then you are yellow, becoming red if the condition persists.

Management Metrics

These metrics should be the most easily quantifiable. The trick here is getting your management to have an attitude of helping rather than using the data for faultfinding. Work that early to have the best chance for success.

▶ **Quality Summary:** No matter what your project type, there should be some quantifiable measure of quality that can be used as a benchmark. Semiconductor design projects often use the rate of change of defects found in the software code as an indication of the quality. Manufacturing projects may use defects per million operations metrics, possibly converting the figure to a sigma number (6 sigma as the goal).

▶ **Schedule/Cost Performance to Goal:** Earned value (EV) was discussed in Chapter 8 and is an excellent source of this metric. You can use CPI/SPI to create one number. If you don't like EV or think it is too complicated, then you are still left with finding some way not just to model schedule performance (BCWP) against goal (BCWS) but also to factor in the actual cost of the work performed (ACWP). Why not just go ahead and implement a simple EV system like the one discussed in Chapter 8?

▶ **Top-Ten-Risks Status Change:** Many project teams have a metric for the top ten risks they face and then play all sorts of games to avoid having to react to the metric. If two or more of your top ten risks move toward greater risk in a given month, then mark this metric yellow. If the yellow risks don't respond to your avoidance plan (drop back to the lower level within two months), raise them to red. You may have to change this metric to zero risks changing as you get closer to project conclusion.

▶ **Procurement Issues:** I include this one because every project these days seems to have major subcontracts or uses pieces of technology from elsewhere. If there is even one procurement issue—current or projected—that is going to impact you elsewhere, then you are yellow. If it persists for two months, you are red.

Team Metrics

Try to surface softer key team issues and to work the quantifiable metrics like labor hours versus plan. Doing so will show your team members you are on their side.

▶ **Space (or similar top team issue):** What does the team

care about? This metric should be the one thing that almost everyone on the project consistently asks about. You should have an existing plan on the issue, with red, yellow, and green status indicators clearly identified.

► **Labor Hours versus Plan:** This metric serves two purposes. First, it tells you how much you are spending in labor per month. Second, you can use it as a proxy to see if you are overworking your people.

► **Percentage of unresolved problems:** You should be keeping a log of problems with SMART goals that the team has asked you to solve. I find that teams don't abuse this, usually bringing up only a handful of problems per year that they themselves cannot solve. If you have one or more problems running over a week late to the plan, you should be yellow. If the problems persist for two straight monthly reporting periods, you are red.

Reporting

Reporting on your project's status is potentially the most dangerous activity you undertake. This is because the people who can affect your career are listening and judging you on the basis of the limited amount of information you present. At the same time, they hear all sorts of things about you and the project from a host of other people. But, if done properly, reporting can become a powerful way to demonstrate strong leadership on your project.

Reporting to Management

Most organizations have monthly reviews, with standard formats for the reporting of project status. These are often called operations or project reviews.

Often project managers get chewed up in these monthly reviews, with many action items of dubious value being assigned by management in a misguided attempt to help. That is the last kind of help you need, right?

But how can you prevent this from occurring? In a nutshell,

you have to appear to be in control of your project. If management thinks things are okay with your project, it will leave you in peace.

Actions You Can Take

Certain specific qualities are necessary to appear in control:

► Be on top of all the facts and data. That is, be able to quickly and succinctly answer any questions management has for you.

► Use good PR management. Management gathers data from all over as it forms its opinion of your performance. By following TACTILE Management leadership principles, you will get good PR from your team, your customer, and others in management.

► Perform well, with few surprises. This is most important, of course. If you hit every schedule milestone (or close), appear to be managing cost and scope well, and anticipate and mitigate risks, management will relax. When it relaxes, it leaves you alone.

There are a few pitfalls to management reporting, most of which have to do with managing management's worries and fears.

Project Pitfall: Management Worrywarts

Disaster projects—projects that have crashed for some reason—can bring out the worst tendencies in management. Managers want this disaster finished, somehow, in any way possible. These projects cause otherwise good senior managers to become obsessive worrywarts.

You may receive kudos if you are the project manager who can finish such a project. You may also lose points if you can't do so. After all, someone (maybe several someones) failed before you, so there must be something fundamentally difficult about the project.

I was once assigned to clean up a disaster project, which had spent a lot of money over several years with no shipped hardware to show for the effort. The first week I was on the project, I began receiving frequent questions from different senior managers via phone call and e-mail. I had a good track record—as you may have—but management tends to worry in the absence of data or visible action. Once it starts to worry, its negative energy can feed on itself, with bad consequences for you.

Even though I had been on the project just a few days, management had a several-years-old itch and wanted it scratched immediately. This often occurs, as perhaps an important manager, often at the behest of a key customer, mandates: "I want this fixed now!"

I knew something had to be done quickly lest I find myself in a daily hour-long meeting being told how to do my job. So I did something very simple. I gave senior managers what they wanted: information about results.

To do this, I sent them daily brief e-mails on our progress, sent early enough that they could read the status report and go home happy, without worry. I stayed at work until I was fairly confident they had all gone home. This cost me a few minutes but saved a lot of aggravation.

These e-mails had an executive summary of no more than three bullet statements, such as, "Unit 4 finished assembly today." Or "Unit 1 finished burn-in today and will ship to the customer on Friday." I am sure that they read only the executive summary, but it was followed by a spreadsheet of unit-by-unit detailed status to show we really had the data.

This report did not take long to write, as I used a standard format, and it helped me focus the effort of the team. I never spent a minute in management's offices taking action items and being told how to manage the project. We shipped as many of the units as we could get to work and closed the project. The customer was glad to have the hardware, and our management had one less headache to deal with. I gained credibility with both groups and was moved on to other assignments.

When I tell this story to groups I sometimes hear, "That wasn't hard. What's so great about that?" My answer is always: "You are right. But it isn't supposed to be hard. By doing that simple daily report, I satisfied management's expectations and dealt with its worries. What was great is that doing so allowed me to have the time and focus to enable the team to do its job." Effective leadership that drives the right results doesn't have to be hard. In fact, if it feels hard, it probably isn't good leadership.

Actions You Can Take

These actions can help ease senior managers' worries and allow you the room you need to do your job:

► Find out what bothers them (see Chapter 5), and give them the data that allays those concerns.

► Being proactive in providing these data will prevent you from being pulled into management "help" sessions. If you do find yourself drawn into those meetings, find ways to define exit criteria so that you can escape. This type of meeting is almost always a huge time waster for everyone.

Project Pitfall: Full-Time Reporting

"We are in trouble on Project XYZ and now management wants daily reports in their offices. We spend an enormous amount of time creating the data for management, and then half the time they don't even have time to attend to them or don't pay attention if they are there. This is the last thing we need right now. All we do is react to management's directives. What can we do?" I have heard that tale of woe many times. "Larry's Tale" in Chapter 5 is one such story.

This is the pit of full-time reporting. The best thing to do is to never get to this point, and you can do that by showing management along the way that you know what you are doing. "Management Worrywarts," the preceding pitfall, contains just such an example.

Actions You Can Take

If you find yourself in the full-time reporting position, do the following:

► Track and then show the number of project people-hours going into the reporting effort. I have even opened separate charge numbers to demonstrate this. Ask what the value is in using that number of hours for that purpose.

► Present an alternative arrangement that will still get management the data it wants. This might be weekly review sessions with daily e-mail updates.

► Work hard to drive down the amount of time involved in all the reporting by questioning the intent of the action items management assigns. Where possible, you should focus management on the goal of the new action item and absorb the new action into existing actions that are geared to solving the same problem.

► Try to get hard dates or accomplished future tasks that will let management stand down from its micromanaging ways.

This is difficult, I know. Senior managers' behavior arises out of desperation and panic. Unspoken is this message: "You didn't do your job, and now we have to do it for you." But if you show them that you are organized, can produce results, and then push firmly but gently to eliminate the full-time reporting, you have a chance to take back your project.

Reporting to Your Customer

In this case, the customer is not the end user of the product or service as, say, you are with your wireless phone but rather the person at the procuring entity's site who is responsible for the contract that pays for your project. Sometimes this person may be in a different part of your larger organization.

In any case, reporting to the customer is likely to be of a contractual nature and thus reflect a formal relationship. You should build a trusting relationship with the customer, nonetheless. That doesn't mean that the customer gets to see all the details of how you and your team make the sausage, but he does get his information from the same set of books as management and your team.

Actions You Can Take

The following actions can help you to build a trusting relationship with your customer:

► Get in the habit of calling the customer and asking him if he has any questions about information in the required project reports.

➤ At periodic reviews, present the truth as it is. Do not play games or try to figure out what the customer wants to hear. Do figure out how to tell him what he needs to hear without losing his ultimate satisfaction.

➤ Ask periodically for feedback, showing action where possible on those issues the customer brings up. Encourage him to come to you first with any complaints. Get in the habit of calling periodically and asking if there are any issues on his end.

Actions like these will build a more trusting relationship with your customers. They may not always be right, but your customers are paying the bills and deserve to be listened to and have their questions answered.

Refer back to Chapter 4 for more insight into how to build a TACTILE relationship with the customer. If you do this from the beginning, you will have laid the solid foundation you need to be able to report honestly and productively to your customer.

Reporting to Your Team

This one is simple but powerful. You report to your team via:

➤ Each weekly key manager's meeting
➤ Each periodic (monthly or quarterly) all-hands meeting
➤ Every interaction you have with anyone on the team

All your actions speak to your team.

Actions You Can Take

Keep these principles in mind as you communicate with your team:

➤ You should tell your team, management, and the customer the same basic data. Don't assume you have to be on message only in team meetings.

➤ Remember, you sell your approach with every interaction. Manage by walking around, making sure you demonstrate the desire to help team members with their issues.

> ➤ Hold "skip-level" one-on-ones to get to know people on your team besides your direct reports.

Case Study: The Path Less Taken

Teams almost never take the time to decide the right bare minimum number of metrics; management often is not connected and doesn't trust project managers and teams; reporting often devolves into full-time reporting. Let's look at these things in action.

Standard Approach

Ravi has driven his people only in the service of technical problems. You will see that his influence over the project and the project stakeholder's is low. He likely finds Deborah and others simply unreasonable, never wondering why this might be the case.

Monitoring

Month 6 of Planned Eighteen-Month Project
CTO Deborah Tabor's Office

"Sebastian. Ravi," Deborah says from behind her desk, not really looking at them. Her tone is lecturing. "As engineering VP and a project manager who have been around here a while, you are both painfully aware that Montane, the project that preceded Alpha Omega, almost killed this design center when it was canceled. I am doing everything in my power to prevent this from happening again. The data that IT has dug up can be used to provide much information. You should apply whatever resources to the effort necessary to generate these new metrics. It is early enough in the project to make a difference." She pauses and looks at them with her direct, cold stare. "How can you not agree?"

Sebastian glances at Ravi with his *don't argue* look.

"There go the extra people I was going to put on the risk mitigation plan for the StackStash." Ravi thinks.

"Are you hiding something, Ravi?" Deborah says impatiently. "Otherwise, why would you not want to take this engineering performance data and use them as a way to watch more closely what is going on in areas like timing?"

"It's fine, Deborah," Ravi replies. "I will get three project controls people on it right away."

Sebastian nods at Deborah. Ravi just stares straight ahead.

Controlling and Reporting

Month 12 of Planned Eighteen-Month Project
Monthly Operations Review
Mahi Mahi Conference Room

They have been discussing the project stoplight chart for an hour now, thirty minutes longer than Ravi scheduled for his entire ops review.

"This appears to me a problem," says Sanjay Singh, the division financial controller. "I do not believe there are no cost implications. This is what these three new engineering metrics show me."

"There probably are," says T.J. Anderson, the division VP for marketing. "But the *desired features* stoplight entry has been red for six months. The customer really wants this."

"You have not made a clear case for new requirements." Sanjay shakes his head stubbornly. "This stoplight entry is a red herring."

"We followed the red-yellow-green criteria agreed to at the gate approval meeting."

"Yes, yes. So what? We cannot afford this, apparently, if the data are to be believed."

Sebastian Turner, the engineering VP, jumps in. "There are now by my count fifty-three entries on Ravi's stoplight chart, at least half of them requested by you all. You can look at any handful in isolation and get any conclusion you want.

"And my conclusion is that we always believe engineering data and we cannot afford this new feature," Sanjay sniffs.

"Not a new feature now," T.J. says, almost sotto voce. "It's just about too late."

Ravi, now having stood mute in front of the room for more than ten minutes, shifts his weight. He sighs quietly and doesn't even try to say anything.

Twenty minutes later, they turn to the next project, not so much having made a decision as just exhausted their collective energy on the topic. The division operations reviews are fifty minutes late to the agenda now. Someone will be briefing very late this evening, as usual.

TACTILE Approach

As you will see, Sheila is effective with all stakeholders because she had a plan coming in on how to do so and has acted consistently on that plan throughout the project.

Monitoring

Month 6 of Planned Eighteen-Month Project
Barracuda Conference Room
Sheila looks across her team of skeptical functional managers. "Yes, that is correct. It is all one set of data. We want to use existing sources of data you are already using as much as possible. We just need schedule work accomplished and the time involved versus the plan, key risks, and performance issues, all of which you work every day and report on each week in our team meetings. Same data are used, maybe in a shorter version, for all other reviews. No extra work; it is the work."

Bennett (never Ben) snorts, "Well, Sheila. You have told us the truth so far, but this I will have to see to believe. Hope you don't mind."

Sheila detects the traces of a slight smile on Bennett's normally quite serious countenance.

Controlling and Reporting

Month 9 of Planned Eighteen-Month Project
Wednesday
Sheila talks with Suresh Kumar, her customer
"Hi, Suresh. This is Sheila Jackson. How are you today? Is this still a good time to talk?"

Suresh Kumar, her customer, about whom Sheila has heard many horror stories concerning how hard he is to work with, answers warmly. "Hello, Sheila. I am quite well today. How are you?"

It has taken a few months, but Suresh no longer looks on her weekly calls with suspicion. At first, he assumed Sheila was hiding problems and asking her three key questions only as a sort of PR move.

"Suresh, I am great as usual. Ran three miles this morning and took my daughter Shannon to a surprisingly interesting version of *The Screwtape Letters* downtown last night. Let me ask you: are there any new problems on your end? Did you have a chance to read the weekly status report I sent last night?"

Suresh pauses for a second or two. He has only glanced at the report. "Let me ask you, Sheila. Is there anything I should be worried about?"

Sheila laughs. "Sure. Any one of several of our top ten risks could jump up and bite us. We are struggling with the SCRAM logic. That's all in the executive summary."

"But none of this has caused you to miss a milestone."

"True, Suresh. So you are okay with things?"

"I am okay with things, Sheila."

"Great. Then let me ask you, did you receive the quarterly design review report that was sent Thursday around midday?"

"Yes."

"Comments?"

"I am working on a few things for you. Nothing major, mostly requesting clarification on what you mean by certain statements."

"Any other concerns with deliverables?"

"Sheila, you ask me this each week. No concerns. I would tell you if there were concerns."

"Great, Suresh. Then how about any worries or emerging problems?"

Suresh pauses. "I do worry a little bit about the SHDMI interface to the StackStash. There is no hard data I can put my finger on, but the jitter on a couple of the signal lines look a lot like problem indicators we have seen on other high-speed interfaces."

Sheila probes Suresh for details on his concerns and writes down everything she learns. The total conversation takes less than ten minutes.

Sheila hurriedly summarizes what she has learned and e-mails it to her functional manager's team under the heading "Customer Potential Emerging Issue." She calls a short meeting so that the team can get its arms around the issue. No one objects. The only other time Sheila called such a meeting, the team discovered that major chunks of logic weren't even getting checked. You better believe the members were going to pay attention to this one.

Month 12 of Planned Eighteen-Month Project
Monthly Operations Review
Mahi Mahi Conference Room

"Here is our stoplight chart, the last chart I have for you." Sheila allows them to look at the ten items on the chart for a moment without comment.

There is something on there of particular interest to everyone in the room. Three of the ten items are yellow. One is red. None of the yellow and red items have been in that status for more than two months. Recovery plans are well under way for each of them.

The red item engenders the most discussion. Because it has been red for two months now, management has a role to play to help. T.J. Anderson receives the action item to talk with the customer's senior management about a requested additional feature that, if added, would have larger cost and schedule impacts than previously thought.

The team discusses the yellow and green items briefly, but no one is overly concerned. Sheila and her team come in every month well prepared; they have not yet missed a schedule milestone. Everything seems in order. Sheila departs, and the group moves on to the next project.

TACTILE Analysis

Sheila's approach has worked. She managed expectations of all key stakeholder groups well and also generated strong business results. Ravi, on the other hand, is really struggling.

Let's compare the approaches taken by Sheila and by Ravi:

▶ **Transparency:** Everything about Sheila is transparent. This is most clearly demonstrated in her call with Suresh, her customer.

Ravi is not deliberately nontransparent; he is just clearly caught up in a culture that makes certain assumptions. He is almost pushed into being nontransparent by the culture in which he must function.

▶ **Accountability:** There is only a kind of *in your face* accountability in the standard example. In the TACTILE example, accountability is displayed on three occasions: (1) Sheila holds herself accountable for what she hears from Suresh; (2) she and her team hold themselves accountable to deal with emergent issues; (3) management holds itself accountable in the ops review to provide help for the red issue.

▶ **Communication:** In the TACTILE example, clear and open communication that is useful for solving problems is clearly demonstrated. In a successful culture that incorporates input from the customer, management, and team, people know what to do and what to expect of others. Such is not the case in the standard example, where several times Ravi is quiet rather than attempting to present a view different from the one being offered; his personal communication is shut down by the culture.

▶ **Trust:** People work together at tasks in Ravi's world, but they don't really trust one another. Look at Deborah Tabor's monologue about what should be done with the newly discovered engineering data for an example of that. In contrast, things go well in Sheila's world because people trust one another. Every action Sheila has taken has been geared toward building this trust, and you can see that it is real.

▶ **Integrity:** As is the case with transparency, no one in the standard example exactly lacks integrity. Rather, everyone ignores the issue and assumes that others may have ulterior motives. In Sheila's world, this is not the case.

▶ **Leadership:** Sheila continues to show the best leadership. No one pushes back against her efforts, while Ravi continually faces micromanagement of one sort or another, along with other obstacles.

▶ **Execution Results:** We see that Sheila's project is cranking right along. There are obstacles to overcome, but the team members do overcome them. Ravi's project just grinds away, careening from one problem to the next, in constant reaction mode. It sure seems like it would be more fun to work in Sheila's world.

Now you can truly see the finish line. You should have some good ideas on how to manage the key phases of your project in an integrated, people-centric way. But, as when you successfully initiate, plan, execute, and monitor a fine birthday party for twenty seven-year-old kids, you still have to put away the left-over food and clean up the dirty dishes. That is what closing is all about. Well, maybe, at least a little bit. Let's move on and finish this so you can get back to your family!

CHAPTER 11

Closing

AFTER MONTHS OF EFFORT, you've finally reached the payoff. Closing is the process of bringing an orderly end to your project, the project that so many people labored over so long. This is not always easy. Organizational fatigue has likely set in, as everyone just wants the project to be finished. The customers want their deliverables. Management wants you to stop spending money. Your people want to get on their next task as soon as possible.

Properly closing and documenting the project's activities is the last thing anyone wants to do. It is all too easy just to do a little window dressing and close the project. Do so, and you are missing a tremendous opportunity. These actions will help you thrive at the end of a project:

➤ Properly close all project activities.

➤ Capture data for organizational learning.

➤ Ensure personal growth.

Properly Close All Project Activities

The process of closing a project seems so simple: "We're done. Close the charge numbers." But, of course, it's not quite that simple. To paraphrase and somewhat simplify the *PMBOK Guide*, you need to (1) finalize the status of all activities; (2) verify, document, and formalize acceptance of the project deliverables; (3) investigate and document the reasons for actions taken if a project has been terminated. Many potential loose ends are implied by those simple words, but let's look at one pitfall: failing to downsize your head-count efficiently and effectively.

Project Pitfall: Resource Discourse

You are really close to the end of the project. Things look pretty good. So let's look at three scenarios. First, the next project wants some of your people—the best, of course. And it wants them now. Some of your team members have approached you and want to stay until the end to get the experience of actually finishing a project. Plus, you need some of them for a thorough closure. What to do?

Second, management wants you to reduce your cost to complete. One way you can do that is by dropping people off the project. But then you worry about getting them back if there is a problem that only they can solve. What to do?

Third, your budget and schedule look good as you cruise in for victory. You have built a pretty good relationship with your key customer. She wants you to keep the right people on board a bit longer than may be necessary just in case her people run into problems fielding the system. What to do?

These three scenarios cover the desires of your team, management, and customer. The tradeoffs are contradictory. There is no clear answer on how to proceed. The best way is to not get overly analytical but to approach the quandary from a values point of view. Yep, values.

Ask yourself some questions, starting with the most quantitative aspect of the issue and proceeding to more qualitative questions.

▶ From a cost point of view, what variance are you projecting? What will keep you out of any penalty box with management? Are you projecting to be under that penalty box number? Then maybe you can afford to keep a few people longer.

▶ What is your overall risk profile? Is risk to completion low? Then maybe you can let a few people leave.

▶ How can you best help your team members grow? Is there a budding project leader whom you might like to groom? Have him manage the closeout. Are there fresh new growth opportunities for others on the team? Maybe you let them go to those opportunities.

▶ Finally, factor all this through your value system and see what answer comes out. Of course, other involved parties will have their own opinions about how to use these people, but at least you will have a firm plan.

It might seem a bit squishy, but this process leads to a much better outcome than would otherwise be the case. I have seen projects jerked back and forth as first one group's demands and then another's drives the decision.

Actions You Can Take

Here's how to avoid getting caught in the crunch of these competing priorities at closing:

▶ Document your approach in detail by team members' names, and discuss with your team and your customer to get their input (not their approval).

▶ Once you have incorporated their thinking, build support within management before you conclude by briefing the closure plan to the right collection of management, probably the project gate approval committee or whatever your organization calls it.

Capture Data for Organizational Learning

Organizations know they need to transfer lessons learned from current to future projects, but often they still do this poorly. They may not make the time or simply are too disorganized to do it properly.

One company that did the post-project process well in my experience was Intel Corporation. Before starting a new project, Intel spent a large number of people-hours discussing a wide range of issues related to fabrication, technology choices, project management approaches, and many other areas in an effort to transfer learning and to learn from mistakes. It also continued this throughout a project's life cycle. When a project ended, an intensive postmortem process took place in an effort to dispassionately identify the problems (and successes) of the project, no matter how potentially embarrassing to a person or to the organization. Learning and improvement were the goals.

Undoubtedly, your organization has a process for this effort. Frequently, organizations use *postmortem* as the term for this effort. I always found this odd, as *postmortem* literally means "after death." I prefer *postpartum*, with its emphasis on "after life." After all, people spend a big chunk of their lives bringing their projects to life, not death. Figure 11-1 helps you simply and efficiently organize your postpartum efforts.

Tool You Can Use: Postpartum One-Pager

The One-Page Postpartum Report increases communication, the one thing that any post-project process is supposed to do. Therefore, it can be used as a summary page for each functional manager in organizations that have no established post-project process, as well as in companies that have extensive processes.

Project name and functional area appear across the top, followed by the manager's name. Each manager should list in bullet form what went well and what didn't go well in his or her functional area. They should then list the other areas and what went well or poorly there. This one-pager is just a summary slide to facilitate discussion. Include as much backup data as needed to support these statements.

Figure 11-1: One-Page Postpartum Report

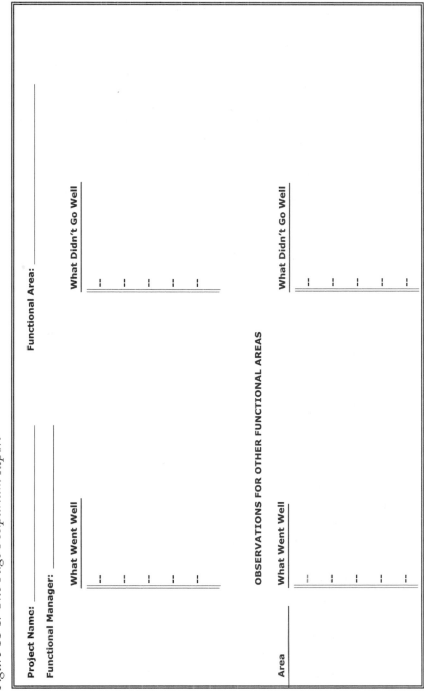

I have seen this type of information presented over multiple days with large collections of individuals involved. I have also seen it presented in cursory form only to management. What I suggest as the most effective way to use these data is to have a key managers meeting (you and your project staff of key functional managers) to discuss, in an open, trusting way, what was learned. This might be a meeting of two to four hours' duration. When the team has its collective arms around the key messages, then have a meeting with the division manager's extended staff, and present the lessons learned with recommendations to that group. Leave no skeletons in the closet. This is the time to highlight what needs to be fixed.

Project Pitfall: The Two-Boat Shuffle

I have observed an interesting phenomenon toward the end of every project I have ever worked on. Unless a plan is created a priori to deal with the phenomenon, virtually everyone on the project begins to plan when he or she can best move from the current project to the next assignment.

The image this brings to mind is that of a person with one foot in each of two boats that are unpredictably wobbling around in the water. The person has to decide the exact second to move from the first boat to the second boat to avoid being left behind or, worse yet, falling into the water.

Actions You Can Take

To keep your team focused on finishing the project at hand:

▶   Be aware that your team members are thinking like this. Work this issue early, and communicate frequently.

▶   To generate a downsizing plan, start meeting with your key managers, and possibly with their teams, to drive the process.

Your project team cannot possibly be working efficiently if it is worrying about which boat to commit to!

Ensure Personal Growth

The most valuable asset that many technology companies have is their intellectual capital, which is just a snooty way of saying their people. So why don't companies spend more time in the post-project period ensuring the personal growth path of at least their most desirable employees from a retention standpoint? "It is your job to manage your career," might be the answer of some companies. That, of course, is shortsighted. A great software designer can manage his career just fine at any one of several other companies that do basically the same work. Keeping him in your company should be everyone's goal and doesn't require that much work. Create a downsizing plan with an eye toward your own personal growth, as well as that of your key functional managers and the rest of the team. I realize you may have to work with, through, and around the HR people (they can also help!) and that most of the team are not your direct employees. Make it work, anyway.

Project Pitfall: Now Let's (Not) Go Change the World

Your project is over. It was a hard fight, but you were successful. You shipped the desired deliverables to the customer when they were promised, maybe only slightly over budget (no one minded), and your team worked well with you the whole way. The project was a real feather in your cap, and you feel good. Remember the lowly 30 to 50 percent project success rate we discussed in Chapter 1. Perhaps you are the only project leader in your organization who truly succeeded.

Now is the time to watch out! Ever hear of hubris? This is not the time to go try to change the entire world.

Actions You Can Take

Just remember a few things and you should be fine:

➤ This is an ongoing process of learning.

➤ Continue to apply your people-based approach to your projects.

> ▶ Be humble. Maybe you were somewhat lucky this time.

> ▶ Don't be arrogant and act like a know-it-all expert entitled to give advice to everyone because you are so smart or because you have *the answer.*

Case Study: The Path Less Taken

There are two approaches to project closing: (1) cut and run, and (2) efficiently closing the project while helping the organization learn and people thrive as they move forward.

Standard Approach

Ravi's approach to closing the project is to spend as little time and effort as possible, to cut and run.

Ensure Personal Growth

Month 16 of Planned Eighteen-Month Project
Ravi Meets with His Key Functional Managers
Sand Shark Conference Room

"So, we agree then." Ravi looks around the room. "We cannot let anyone go to Beta Grande, except for a few of the poorest performers, and they won't want them."

They all nod in satisfaction.

Later that day…
Ravi Talks with Sharon Narvon, Project Leader for BTC's Newest Project

"That is correct, Sharon. We have only these ten or so people we can release at this point. We are behind. I am sure you understand that."

"But, Ravi, we are not ramping up properly. And these people you are releasing do not help me." She pauses. "Ah, this is . . . what is the word? Disgusting. Yes, that is the word. You are disgusting me. We will not get a good start because you are late. This never stops in this company." She pauses again, waiting for Ravi to speak. He says nothing.

"I will talk to Deborah." Sharon sighs. "Perhaps she will see reason."

Ravi laughs slightly. "Go ahead. If she takes the people we need to finish, then I will have an explanation for why we are late."

"Yes, what you say is probably true. And then BTC suffers."

Ravi says nothing.

Properly Close All Project Activities and Capture Data for Organizational Learning

Month 20 of Planned Eighteen-Month Project
Ravi Meets with His Key Functional Managers
Tilapia Conference Room

"We will close them all, except for support. I will open a new department number for ongoing support. You may all charge that department for the rest of the month. After that, your own department will have to carry you until a new project assignment comes up. I want to see an immediate ramp-down plan for the rest of your people. None of them on the charge numbers after next week."

Bennett (never Ben) Lee looks hard at Ravi. "Thanks for holding onto everyone for so long. My best designer left for Intel last week because she was afraid she would miss out on Beta Grande."

Lance nods. "I've lost a couple of folks, too."

Ravi has no sympathy for them. "We lose some people, we get some people. This is how we run our projects. You know this. Quit your grumbling."

"How about postmortem?" Jiao Lee, the design assurance manager, asks, interested in fixing some of the problems for future projects. Zev Cohen, verification manager, and Rajesh Kumar, DFT manager, nod vigorously. Their functions will benefit enormously if recurrent problems are fixed.

Ravi shakes his head. "This will be minimal. We have no money for doing a big song and dance about what went wrong. Follow the corporate procedure, spending as little time as you can. We will cover it in a staff meeting sometime."

Ensure Personal Growth (Again)

One week later …
Project Conclusion, Two Months Late
Ravi Meets with Sebastian
Sebastian's Office

"We were lucky to finish two months late, Sebastian."

"That's not how management sees it, Ravi. They are taking a hard line on missing market windows."

Ravi is incredulous. "So, what are you saying? After working my ass off for almost fifteen years, working a hundred hours a week on Alpha Omega, and getting it done by hook or by crook, I am to be punished?"

"You still have your grade, your pay rate, and your options plan. You can use a little break, anyway. What's to worry? Getting back into design, running a small team will probably be fun for you. More time for your family."

Ravi just stares at him. "My family has learned how to be busy without me. And the rest of the staff, my functional managers?"

Sebastian shrugs, then breaks eye contact and looks out the window. "Don't worry about it. Most of them are on Beta Grande, one way or the other. No one comes out ahead when you are late. It's the new world order."

Ravi follows Sebastian's gaze. He sees nothing that reassures him.

TACTILE Approach

Sheila's approach to closing the project (as shown below) is quite different from Ravi's. Her approach is better for her people and better meets the needs and expectations of her organization.

Properly Close All Project Activities

Month 16 of Planned Eighteen-Month Project
Barracuda Conference Room

Sheila looks out at the group. "This week we start a new agenda item." She pauses to let that sink in. "We are going to spend a few minutes, no more than about thirty each week, talking about transitioning the project to conclusion: shutting charge numbers in a logical and thoughtful way; planning the post-project—which I call postpartum, by the way—properly; and figuring out what to do with all of us after the project. Questions?"

She patiently answers all their questions, snide comments, and cynical asides.

Ensure Personal Growth

Month 17 of Planned Eighteen-Month Project
Sebastian's Office

Sheila and Sebastian look at each other. "That's it, then?" Sebastian asks with satisfaction.

"Yep. These people can go now, and the ones on the right can go on the dates you see. We are pretty much finished with them, as long as we can get them back if there is a major problem."

Sebastian hesitates and says, "Yes, you can trust me on that, Sheila."

She looks at him. "I know. Now, moving on to the next item."

Capture Data for Organizational Learning

One week after project tape-out (finished design sent to manufacturing)…

Postpartum Planning Meeting with Key Functional Managers
Barracuda Conference Room

"You all have what you need to finish your post-partum one-pagers, right?" Sheila surveys the room visually. Everyone nods, even Bennett and Lance. Jiao, Rajesh, and Zev are beaming.

Sheila smiles. "Good. Next week we will share them with one another. That will be the longest agenda item for our staff meeting. The week after, we will talk about cross-functional issues. Then, the next week we will have a two-hour meeting with Mark and his staff to review our findings. Make sense?"

Everyone nods.

Ensure Personal Growth (Again)

One month after project tape-out…

Sebastian's Office

"You're sure this is the role you want, Sheila?"

Sheila nods vigorously.

"Organizational coach for the project leaders and staff? What kinds of career progression can that enable?"

"The ones that are good for me, where my interests, passions, and talents intersect with a need BTC has."

Sebastian nods flatly. "Sure, I can see that we need this. But you are going to meet a lot of inertia, some passive and some active resistance." He looks at her.

"Unlike on Alpha Omega, you mean?" Sheila asks, smiling.

Sebastian grins at her. "That's right."

"That works for me. Now, moving on. Here is where we were last time we talked on the rest of the functional managers. Most of them are already on Beta Grande, have been for various amounts of time. Now, about Bennett. I have just the job for him . . ."

TACTILE Analysis

I will forgo a detailed discussion of each of the seven characteristics here in favor of a look at the big picture. At the end of this case study, the divergent approaches have led to vastly different results, both for the project and for the teams.

Ravi is lost in his task list, driving his team with little empathy. He doesn't view his approach as anything bad. His lack of transparency, his ham-fisted way of trying to hold people accountable, and his overall poor communications skills do not drive trust with any of his key stakeholder groups.

If asked, people who work with him closely every day would quite possibly agree that he is an honest guy just doing his job. They probably like him. But that isn't good enough when you are leading teams of people, interacting closely with customers who may be far away, and with management that may be distracted but still demands results.

Ravi has poor people skills. Many technology companies do not truly value these so-called soft skills. I hope that you now see that these skills are in fact vitally important. The business results that Ravi generated are about par for the course. The project is late but finished. The people have new jobs but continue exhausted. Management, possibly not very good at the right kinds of leadership itself, desperately seeks someone who can generate different results with the same old approaches and culture. We can have so much more.

Sheila may seem like an impossibly wonderful person, made up by this writer to illustrate what to some of you are squishy concepts too abstract to be useful in the real world. But I know many people who try to manage this way. Organizations just don't seek them out enough for the kinds of project leader jobs we are discussing, preferring so-called technical experts, who fall short in so many other ways.

Sheila displays transparency and seeks to establish accountability and to communicate clearly in all her efforts. She builds trust with her customer, her management, and her team. All of this is based on her personal integrity. Her leadership style is what experts increasingly are suggesting as the right kind of leadership. Her business results are excellent. She finishes on time without burning out her team; she plans well for their future, enables organizational learning, and closes her project effectively and efficiently.

I think TACTILE Management will help you do the same.

PART V:
Living Well in the Project Management Jungle

CHAPTER 12

"From Chaos Comes Creativity, from Order Comes Profit"

IT IS 9:15 P.M., a Tuesday night like any other. A light burns inside a beautiful Tudor-style custom home on the edge of the Northwest Hills in Austin, Texas. Inside, yet another busy knowledge-worker team project manager finishes up his work for the day, an e-mail of congratulations to his team on making its most recent milestone.

In response, he receives an e-mail of appreciation from Dave, his supervisor, before he signs off. Down the hall, his two children slumber away. Five and three years old, they are the light of his life. He glances inside their room as he walks toward the master bedroom. Happily, he remembers the tickets in his wallet for Saturday's upcoming performance of "Elmo on Ice."

As he opens the master bedroom door, he sees his wife reading in bed. She smiles as he comes into the room. "Got some energy left for me?" she asks. He nods and grins back at her.

He turns his cell phone off for the night as he changes into his sleepwear. He has a planned call with his Asian customer for 5 A.M. Since the project is doing so well, he expects it to be the usual short pro forma call.

The quotation used as the title of this chapter comes from Robert I. Sutton's blog, "Work Matters," for March 1, 2010, at www.psychologytoday.com. If you recall all the way back to the beginning of Chapter 1, you may remember a similar fellow caught up in the chaos, with very different results. Our friend in Chapter 1 had no time for his family; he was working around the clock and still couldn't seem to produce the desired results.

Follow the TACTILE Management approach, and the satisfying and profitable results described at the beginning of this chapter will be yours—even on the exact same projects that would have driven you to distraction had you done them the same old way.

TACTILE Management is not a new process in the fashion of Agile or Lean. Sadly, business too often today seems to demand quick answers that can be used like some sort of medicine to solve all the organization's problems. The thinking seems to be "Send everyone to a class, get them a colored belt, and your organization will be fine, too." These quick-fix approaches don't work because they don't change the culture and they don't work through people's expectations.

TACTILE takes a different view. TACTILE Management is a toolbox of approaches to apply no matter what process you are using. They are successful because they work through people and their needs, wants, and desires. Let's briefly go through the toolbox.

First are the seven characteristics discussed in Chapter 2 that form the philosophical base of TACTILE Management: transparency, accountability, communication, trust, integrity, leadership that drives needed change, and execution results. These are the values that drive my actions, and I believe that the right values can help you succeed. But what, if any, role do values play in business, or is it just cutthroat *every person for himself?* If so, where does that Darwinian approach actually get you? Does it work in the long run? Does it lead to real success? In the past few years, we've seen a lot of very public examples, in the world of finance, in the car industry, and in others, where the lack of these values—transparency, accountability, communication, and other TACTILE characteristics—has led to some epic downfalls.

Second is the Expectations Pyramid, discussed in Chapters 3–6. Most project managers spend too much time focusing on the technical aspects of the project and try to control the project through the traditional triple constraints of performance, schedule, and cost. They essentially ignore the people aspects of the project or relegate them to "touchy-feely HR issues that we don't have time for." TACTILE Management adds the expectations of your customer, management, and team as three people-based constraints.

Third, we showed in Chapters 7–11 how to apply the seven TACTILE characteristics and the Expectations Pyramid in the five project phases of initiating, planning, executing, monitoring and controlling, and closing.

At its heart, TACTILE Management is centered on people. These tools are all just ways to help you, the project manager, sharpen your focus where it needs to be—not on chasing the next looming deadline and then the next one or endlessly striving for and failing to reach unrealistic goals set by someone else, but on *people.* All projects are the product of individuals, each with his or her own needs, expectations, and goals.

The TACTILE approach shows you that by developing and implementing your own set of values to drive your actions, you can unite these people to target one goal—the team's goal. TACTILE Management, because it focuses on these people issues, can thus be used with any project management tool or process to drive the business results you are looking for. Then your team will thrive, your company will thrive, and you will thrive.

Bibliography

Annunzio, Susan Lucia. *Contagious Success: Spreading High Performance throughout Your Organization*. New York: Portfolio, 2004.

Bennis, Warren, Daniel Goleman, and James O Toole. *Transparency: How Leaders Create a Culture of Candor*. With Patricia Ward Biederman. San Francisco: Jossey-Bass, 2008.

Bossidy, Larry, and Ram Charan. *Execution: The Discipline of Getting Things Done*. New York: Crown Business, 2002.

Boulding, Kenneth. "General Systems Theory: The Skeleton of Science." *Management Science* 2, no. 3 (April 1956): 197–208.

Carter, Stephen L. *Integrity*. New York: HarperPerennial, 1997.

Chiles, James R. *Inviting Disaster*. New York: HarperBusiness, 2002.

Collins, Jim. *Good to Great: Why Some Companies Make the Leap . . . and Others Don't*. New York: HarperCollins, 2001.

Connors, Roger, and Tom Smith. *How Did That Happen?: Holding People Accountable for Results the Positive, Principled Way*. New York: Portfolio, 2009.

Covey, Stephen P. *The 8th Habit: From Effectiveness to Greatness*. New York: Free Press, 2004.

Crouch, Alfred L. *Design for Test for Digital IC's and Embedded Core Systems*. Upper Saddle River, N.J.: Prentice Hall PTR, 1999

Davis, David. "Beware of False Economies." *Harvard Business Review on Managing Projects*. Boston: Harvard Business School Press, 2005.

DeMarco, Tom, and Timothy Lister. *Peopleware: Productive Projects and Teams*. New York: Dorset House, 1987.

Duarte, Nancy. *slide:ology: The Art and Science of Creating Great Presentations*. Sebastopol, Calif.: O'Reilly, 2008.

Fleming, Quentin W., and Joel M. Hoppelman. *Earned Value Project Management*. Newton Square, Penn.: Project Management Institute, 1996.

Goldratt, Eliyahu M. *Critical Chain*. Great Barrington, Mass.: North River Press, 1997.

Goleman, Daniel. *Emotional Intelligence: 10th Anniversary Edition; Why It Can Matter More Than IQ*. New York: Bantam 2006.

———. *Social Intelligence: The New Science of Human Relationships*. New York: Bantam, 2006.

Goodwin, Doris Kearns. *Team of Rivals: The Political Genius of Abraham Lincoln*. New York: Simon & Schuster, 2005.

Greater Devine Chamber of Commerce. "Devine History." http://www.devinechamber.com/history.html (accessed February 2010).

Hesselbein, Frances, Marshall Goldsmith, and Iain Somerville, eds. *Leading beyond the Walls*. San Francisco: Jossey-Bass. 1999.

Hesselbein, Frances. *Hesselbein on Leadership*. San Francisco: Jossey-Bass, 2002.

Highsmith, Jim. *Agile Project Management: Creating Innovative Products*. Boston: Addison-Wesley. 2004.

Hughes, Marcia, and James Bradford Terrell. *The Emotionally Intelligent Team: Understanding and Developing the Behaviors of Success*. San Francisco: Jossey-Bass, 2007.

Johnson, Richard A., Fremont E. Kast, and James E. Rosenzweig. *The Theory and Management of Systems*. 2nd ed. New York: McGraw-Hill, 1967.

Kendrick, Tom. *Results without Authority: Controlling a Project When the Team Doesn't Report to You*. New York: AMACOM, 2006.

Kerzner, Harold. *Project Management: A Systems Approach to Planning, Scheduling, and Controlling*. 6th ed. New York: Wiley, 1998.

Krzyzewski, Mike. *Leading with the Heart: Coach K's Successful Strategies for Basketball, Business and Life*. With Donald T. Phillips. New York: Warner Books, 2001.

———. *The Gold Standard: Building a World-Class Team*. With Jamie K. Spatola. New York: Business Plus, 2009.

Lencioni, Patrick. *The Five Dysfunctions of a Team: A Leadership Fable*. San Francisco: Jossey-Bass, 2002.

Lombardo, Michael M., and Robert W. Eichinger. *FYI for Your Improvement*. 4th ed. Minneapolis: Lominger International, 2006.

Matta, Nadim F., and Ronald N. Ashkenas. "Why Good Projects Fail Anyway." *Harvard Business Review on Managing Projects*. Boston: Harvard Business School Press, 2005.

McFarland, Grant. *Microprocessor Design: A Practical Guide from Design Planning to Manufacturing*. New York: McGraw-Hill, 2006.

McKay, Judy. *Managing the Test People: A Guide to Practical Technical Management*. Santa Barbara, Calif.: Rocky Nook, 2007.

Mersino, Anthony C. *Emotional Intelligence for Project Managers: The People Skills You Need to Achieve Outstanding Results*. New York: AMACOM, 2007.

Nadler, Reldan S. *The Leaders' Playbook: How to Apply Emotional Intelligence—Keys to Great Leadership*. Edited by Ilene Segalove. Santa Barbara, Calif.: Psyccess Press, 2007.

National Instruments. "Company Overview." http://www.ni.com/company/ (accessed November 2009).

Phillips, Donald T. *Lincoln on Leadership: Executive Strategies for Tough Times*. New York: Warner Books, 1992.

Project Management Institute. *A Guide to the Project Management Body of Knowledge: PMBOK Guide*. 3rd ed. Newton Square, Penn: Project Management Institute, 2004.

Rath, Tom. *StrengthsFinder 2.0*. New York: Gallup Press, 2007.

Robinson, B. A. "Shared Belief in the 'Golden Rule' (a.k.a. Ethics of Reciprocity)." April 2, 2010. http://www.religioustolerance.org/reciproc.htm (accessed May 2010).

Royer, Isabelle. "Why Bad Projects are so Hard to Kill." *Harvard Business Review on Managing Projects*. Boston: Harvard Business School Press, 2005.

Ruffa, Stephen A. *Going Lean: How the Best Companies Apply Lean Manufacturing Principles to Shatter Uncertainty, Drive Innovation, and Maximize Profits*. New York: AMACOM, 2008.

State Farm. "2010 State Farm Code of Conduct." http://www.statefarm.com/about/media/intro_code.asp (accessed February 2010).

Sutton, Robert I. "From Chaos Comes Creativity, from Order Comes Profit." March 1, 2010. http://www.psychologytoday.com/blog/work-matters /201003 /chaos-comes-creativity-order-comes-profit (accessed May 2010).

Townsend, Robert. *Up the Organization: How to Stop the Corporation from Stifling People and Strangling Profit*. San Francisco: Jossey-Bass, 2007.

U.S. Securities and Exchange Commission. "NATIONAL INSTRUMENTS CORP /DE/ - FORM 10-Q - October 27, 2009." http://www.faqs.org/sec-filings/091027 /NATIONAL-INSTRUMENTS-CORP-DE-_10-Q/ (accessed November 2009).

Waugh, John C. *Lincoln and McClellan: The Troubled Partnership between a President and his General*. New York: Palgrave Macmillan, 2010.

Wikipedia. "George Armstrong Custer." http://en.wikipedia.org/wiki/George_Armstrong_Custer (accessed April 2009).

Wooden, John R., and Jay Carty. *Coach Wooden's Pyramid of Success*. Ventura, Calif.: Regal, 2005.

Index